SHYLOCK
FOR A SUMMER

Frederick Valk

SHYLOCK
FOR A SUMMER

*The story of one year (1954-5) in the
life of Frederick Valk*

BY DIANA VALK

with notes by
TYRONE GUTHRIE *and* DONALD DAVIS

WITH FRONTISPIECE AND 8 PP OF HALF-TONE ILLUSTRATIONS

CASSELL · LONDON

CASSELL & COMPANY LTD

35 Red Lion Square, London, WC1

and at

210 Queen Street, Melbourne
26/30 Clarence Street, Sydney
24 Wyndham Street, Auckland
1068 Broadview Avenue, Toronto 6
PO Box 275, Cape Town
PO Box 11190, Johannesburg
Haroon Chambers, South Napier Road, Karachi
13/14 Ajmeri Gate Extension, New Delhi 1
15 Graham Road, Ballard Estate, Bombay 1
17 Chittaranjan Avenue, Calcutta 13
PO Box 23, Colombo
Macdonald House, Orchard Road, Singapore 9
Avenida 9 de Julho 1138, São Paulo
Galeria Güemes, Escritorio 454/59 Florida 165, Buenos Aires
Marne 5b, Mexico 5, DF
Sanshin Building, 6 Kanda Mitoschiro-cho, Chiyoda-ku, Tokyo
25 rue Henri Barbusse, Paris 5e
25 Ny Strandvej, Espergaerde, Copenhagen
Beulingstraat 2, Amsterdam-C
Bederstrasse 51, Zürich 2

PRINTED IN GREAT BRITAIN BY THE SHENVAL PRESS
LONDON, HERTFORD AND HARLOW
F. 358

CONTENTS

LIST OF ILLUSTRATIONS

AUTHOR'S NOTE

Among notes and diaries for a record of his life which
FREDERICK VALK long intended writing himself are
these words:

> I don't want to talk at length of my histrionic
> adventures—the idea of this is to draw the curve of a
> life, lived in shadow and sun but lived with grateful-
> ness.

The story in this book attempts to carry out his idea. It was
planned in something like its present form, as a record for
our two young sons of their first visit to Canada. It is
dedicated to the Stratford Shakespearean Festival of
Ontario and all those who take part in it.

DIANA VALK

ACKNOWLEDGMENTS

My thanks are due to the Empire Club of Canada for its kind permission to reprint the address 'Theatre in Europe and the Americas' and to Mr Robertson Davies and the *Peterborough Examiner, Ontario*, for permission to use the obituary notice of Frederick Valk; to Mr Don McKague, Mr John Steele, Mr Oswald Wild and the *Beacon-Herald*, Stratford, Ontario, for permission to reproduce the photographs in this book and to Mrs Joan Gascoyne for her unfailing help and encouragement with the manuscript.

D. V.

FREDERICK VALK

BY TYRONE GUTHRIE

I first saw Frederick Valk act in a piece called *Thunder Rock*. He played a doctor, and gave the impression, which is one of the hall-marks of top-flight acting, not of being just a particular doctor, but of the Idea of Medicine; he was an archetype of Doctor.

We met about two years later in connexion with a production of *Othello* by the Old Vic. This was his second Shakespearean part in English, and the language was a major difficulty. But there was no mistaking the majestic size and power of the performance, a bigness of conception which matched his remarkable physical equipment. I shall always regret that no opportunity came for him to play *King Lear* in English.

The physical attributes of all of us are important determinants of our character and destiny. But it is possible to conceive that a man of any size or shape might do well as a dentist. He need not look like a dentist, because there is no public preconception of what a dentist ought to look like. But this is not always the case. A hero is certainly expected to look heroic and yet it doesn't matter too much if he looks, as so many heroes do, like a nervous spinster. Indeed, many of the great figures of history present a very unexpected appearance. A person with the physical attributes of Julius Caesar or Napoleon Bonaparte would look like a bar-tender or a bank clerk, but could never be envisaged as a great conqueror.

But an actor must, to a certain extent, embody the popular conception of what he is playing. If he looks like a nervous spinster he will, except on the rarest occasion, be cast as a nervous spinster. Valk's physique was remarkable and greatly determined his career in the theatre.

The illustrations in this book give some striking impressions of his appearance. But let me amplify these impressions by trying to describe what I remember.

He was of somewhat more than middle height, but the head and chest were those of a giant; and the limbs seemed by comparison rather short and thick; the whole effect was immensely powerful but squat. A great head on a great barrel, round, incredibly thick, but not fat: hard, not soft. The face, like the whole figure, was broad in comparison with its length; wide-set eyes, a short thick nose, a wide mouth and very square jaw. The neck was short and immensely thick. But any impression of coarseness was immediately obliterated by the eyes, the directness of their glance, the candour and intelligence of their expression, their extraordinary and benevolent magnetism. His colouring was extremely swarthy; dark, but not black hair; a darkly sallow complexion quite unlike the ruddy colouring of a robust Briton; the eyes were a warm bright brown and, for all their brilliance, the 'white' of the eyes was not white at all, but like dark ivory.

It is often the case that extremely powerful men have silly, squeaky little voices. Valk's voice matched his physique; a warm and velvety baritone with an upper register of extraordinary brilliance and power. Probably it was due to the gigantic muscular development of the diaphragm, but I do not think I have ever heard a man's voice which had the same ringing, uninhibited power at the top.

It is impossible to assess his talent in comparison with other leading actors in the English-speaking theatre, because English was not his first language. In spite of heroic efforts he never entirely mastered the illogical intricacies of English pronunciation. Inevitably, therefore, his English-speaking career was restricted to roles in which 'an accent' was permissible. Unfortunately, this seriously restricted the great classical parts for which he was otherwise so suitable, and which he so dearly longed to play.

But, as always, nature takes away with one hand and with the other offers compensation. I think the great setback to his career, the painful adjustment to being a refugee, developed his character, made him the man he was, more thoughtful, gentle, humble, and wise than the great star he might, in other circumstances, have been.

Apart from the language, he had to adapt himself to the style of the English-speaking stage. In Central Europe acting is larger, louder, more uninhibited; more emphasis is placed upon the virtuosity of the soloist and less upon the values of teamwork. Frederick Valk made this adaptation well. He was a fine member of a team, and always placed the meaning of the play before any opportunity which might permit him to score individually. His chief fault as an actor, in my opinion, was a tendency to rush at an emotional scene like a bull at a gate. It was hard for him to control the powerful torrent of his own feeling, the trombone tones of that great voice, and to build up a climax by slow degrees, step by disciplined step. On the other hand he preserved from his old training a splendid technical breadth and freedom in the use of both the voice and the whole body. This was one of the reasons why I was so anxious that he should work with the Canadian Company at Stratford.

Canadian actors, trained largely in the radio and in TV studios, accustomed to the extremely narrow limits which microphone and camera impose, accustomed more to the intimate demands of modern naturalistic plays than to the wider imaginative and technical scope of great classics, do not readily lay their ears back and roar, cannot without self-consciousness make the broad and vehement gestures which match vehement declamation. Until Valk came they had not worked alongside a great, white, spouting whale.

What he brought to Canada of the European classical tradition has been a valuable and enriching new element. It was assimilated by the Canadian actors and has become, I believe, a part of the incipient Canadian tradition, a part of what the senior actors year by year impart, by example, to the newcomers. What he brought was assimilable, partly because the Canadians are bright enough to know a good thing when they see it, but even more because Freddie Valk made no attempt to instruct or to Know Best, but merely allowed his knowledge and his craft to speak for themselves. He was older than most, if not all, of his fellow players. But this was not a barrier, rather the reverse. One of the features of his character was his love and reverence for all young growing things—be they people or animals or plants, or a young country like Canada, or a young institution like the Canadian Shakespeare Festival.

We mourn the fact that this genial, gentle giant is no longer physically present in our midst; but those of us, who knew him and loved him, are glad that this intimate, humorous, unpretentious chronicle of that happy and fruitful time in Canada will enable others to share part of our memory.

A TRIBUTE

BY DONALD DAVIS

Shylock for a Summer is not a conventional biography, as you will see. It is not concerned with giving an itinerary of a great actor's career. It tells rather of a great man and a great spirit. By recalling the essence of a vital year in his life (and which year was not vital?), Mrs Valk has evoked to an incredible degree the personal magnetism, strength, humour, and understanding, the essential goodness and humanity of Frederick Valk.

It was not until May of 1955, in Stratford, Ontario, that I met Freddie, at a reception given by the Board of Governors of the Festival Foundation for the members of the acting company who were just commencing rehearsals. I had seen him on the stage only once—a performance of *The Same Sky* in London in 1952. Yet, from the moment he entered the room on a hot summer afternoon literally minutes after his arrival in Stratford, we seemed to be 'with' Freddie. There was no constraint, no probationary period of getting-to-know 'the Star'. The simple act of walking through the door was apparently sufficient. He seemed immediately to have become one of the company, eager to begin work—new work, with new people in yet another new country. Spontaneously he embraced us all with an affectionate bear-hug of vitality and enthusiasm, as he was shortly to embrace his Canadian audiences. He belonged to us. Only later did one come to wonder whether the reverse was not nearer to the truth—that we belonged to him!

I cannot view *Shylock for a Summer* dispassionately, because during the months that Freddie spent in Stratford and Toronto, I was privileged to be closely associated with him. He seemed to grasp intuitively the problems and potentials of theatre in Canada. In some extraordinary way he became a catalyst giving form and resolution to our work, like some benign Svengali willing us to see and strive for an ideal—both as artists and as people. Despite the personal involvement, however, I feel certain that the reader, whether theatrically inclined or not, will find himself completely absorbed by this account of an artist who in his life-time achieved success not in one, but two careers—this account of a man who had seen every value in his life irrevocably destroyed, and who somewhere found the strength and courage to create a new life for himself. Underlying the whole, one is deeply moved by the wonderful relationship which existed between Freddie and Diana Valk. Beyond a doubt, here is the well-spring from which Freddie drew his strength and purpose.

Frederick Valk was born in Hamburg, Germany, on June 10, 1895. He died in London on July 23, 1956, during the run of *Romanoff and Juliet* by Peter Ustinov, in which he was enjoying a great popular success. I do not mourn Freddie in the conventional sense; his memory is far too vital for that. I do regret, however, that the public knew so little of Frederick Valk, the comedian. His fame as an actor, both in Europe and in Great Britain, was based on his interpretation of the 'heavy' roles, the villains and tragic heroes, so antithetical to the man. His abundant humour (that wonderful twinkle behind his eyes which on the stage often threatened to break forth at disconcertingly serious moments!) and his superlative sense of comedy were never fully exploited in the theatre. At the time of his death, Freddie had accepted an offer to go to New York for the American production of *Romanoff and Juliet*. In Toronto, my brother and I were already planning for his return to Canada and the Crest at the close of his Broadway run. Ibsen's *John Gabriel Borkman*, we thought, is a must, and a comedy . . . Freddie had died before I saw *The Waltz of the Toreadors;* I would have given much to have seen his General St. Pé.

PART 1

EUROPE

1

JOURNEY INTO THE PAST

This is to be the story of one year in the life of an actor's family—father, mother and two small boys—not indeed the calendar year according to custom, but a period in time which stands by itself. This year was too much for any ordinary calendar, so rich in experience and varied in events that it had to take on an extra month or so to cover the highspots between early fall 1954 and December 1955.

By a chain of circumstances completely unforeseen these few months linked together the whole of Frederick Valk's life as a Shakespearean actor and it is therefore necessary, in the early pages of this book, to leave Britain where he made his home and to go back with him in time, to Hamburg, Munich, Berlin, and Stuttgart in Germany, so as to be able to pick up these links with the past which bear directly on the work he was able to do in the Canadian Theatre.

It may be asked why should anyone journey into the past in order to go to Canada, why not just go? But this story deals with the sequence of events as they came about and these events laid the foundation and set the stage for our Canadian visit. The discovery, in Europe, that the past was finally the past was perhaps made possible for

Freddie by the fact that he was committed to go to Canada, certainly it released in him an immense store of energy which, with the knowledge he had accumulated over the years, could be put to work for a theatre active for the future.

The year did not open with a lead to follow any new road, it began with a visit to Germany, where Freddie was born, where he grew up and was trained as an actor and made his name. More often than not, by word of mouth and in the Press, Freddie was described as a Czech. He did become a Czech citizen before the outbreak of the Second World War and this was the freak chance which led him to a career in the English-speaking world. At the time of the Munich crisis and for several months after, no visas were needed between Czechoslovakia and Britain, while nearly all the other European countries had passport restrictions, and the journey from Prague to London is only a matter of hours. But Freddie was born a North German, not a Slav. His father came from the little town of Emden, more nearly Dutch in character than German, with its windmills, dykes, and Holstein cattle, and his family, with a name more Dutch than German, was, it is thought, of Portuguese-Jewish extraction. His mother hailed from Mecklenburg and the family lived and worked in Hamburg.

In late October 1954, not thinking of Shakespeare or his plays, Freddie flew out to Bavaria to take part in a movie. This trip was only his second visit to Germany since he left for Czechoslovakia to make his home in Prague as leading actor in the German-speaking theatre.

He did not return till he went over from Britain after the war, having spent six years in Prague and nearly seven in the British Isles. We had set up house in London and our elder son, William, was three months old when his father was invited to broadcast the part of Galileo in a radio version of Berthold Brecht's play, to be broadcast by the North-West German Radio in the British Zone of Germany. This radio-station was at that time under the control of the BBC and to accept the engagement meant a three weeks' stay in Hamburg.

Going back to the old country is at all times a tricky business for those who have been forced to emigrate by a hostile political machine. At no time can it be a pleasure trip. Freddie accepted Berthold Brecht's distinguished play willingly enough, the part of Galileo appealed to him and it was his first dramatic role in the German language for nine years. The big political speeches of the war, of Churchill, Roosevelt, and Stalin, had been broadcast to Germany by his voice speaking through the BBC but that was not the equivalent of a dramatic role.

The offer came very late at night and he viewed the journey with some misgiving. We went up to look at the sleeping baby; there was little to be seen of him apart from a determined crest of silky hair. Never, said his father, never should this child become a German citizen. Yet here was now the chance, which must come sooner or later, for Freddie to see for himself what had become of his former country through Hitler, and he decided to go to Hamburg, to visit Berlin, if time allowed, and to look up his old friends. Should we all three go together? No, he said, not with a three months' old baby, in midwinter, not there.

Hamburg was to be his headquarters. This proudest and wealthiest of the Hanseatic towns was first remembered by him as the place where, at three years old, he ran away from home one evening during a military parade. Torchlight, glittering on the horses' harness, on the helmets of the cavalrymen and on their lances, attracted the little boy and he was delighted with the band, so that he went dodging in and out between the horses' hooves in search of the Emperor—no lesser man would do. In the end a policeman spotted him blinking at the street lights, a figure in a sailor-suit, smaller than any sailor, in this town of sailors, had any right to be. The child was put under benevolent arrest at the nearest police-station and fed on bread-and-butter till his parents could be found and taken to task for allowing him to roam the streets alone.

Hamburg had been Freddie's home town for thirty years before ever he had any idea of becoming a Czech citizen and before Czechoslovakia existed as an independent state. As a boy whose home was in one of the greatest sea-ports of the world the name of Prague meant nothing more to him than the final destination of long chains of barges plying up the river Elbe, freight-barges of a design peculiar to this river, built so that they could travel all the way upstream from Hamburg to that mysterious city on the borderlands of the Austro-Hungarian Empire. Describing Hamburg as he saw it later on, exploring with three other boys, his school-friends, Freddie wrote:

A beautiful city, a forest of ship-cranes, masts, ships and their huge funnels. In rain and fog and ice, every season gave its own poetry to the harbour, to the busy launches, to the booming ocean liners. All the spices of the seven seas were ours with the odours of rotting wood and seaweed, our haunts were in the old city, the little unswept streets of old Hamburg, where the ancient half-timbered houses leaned towards us, reflecting the autumn sunlight from their windows. The glittering river Elbe rolled towards the North Sea, broad and majestical and beyond the river, beyond the woods lay the wide distances of the Lüneburg heath, a kingdom for friends to enjoy. All that and church spires, Saint Michealis towering above the old city, copper-green in the onion style of the eighteenth century, in contrast to Saint Petri whose spire shot up into the sky like a spear cutting a huge triangular hole in the backdrop of the heaven, like the entrance to a tent.

Saint Petri overlooked the river Alster, more like an inland lake than a river—Saint Petri guarded the Maidens' Walk, the city's pride. There were the elegant shops, hotels and banking-houses on one side of the street, on the other was just a comfortable embankment with the burghers' national café, the Alsterpavilion, as its crowning glory.

It was a gay affair, this Alsterpavilion, with rows of chairs and tables and multi-coloured giant umbrellas outdoors and crowds of Hambourgeois well-mixed with foreigners, actors and the gilded youth of Hamburg— children of good families, flaxen-haired, greatly impressed by their own distinction and quality, though at times indistinguishable from those of humbler stock—all sitting there overlooking the Alster's many rowing-boats and little white steamers. A beautiful city where the people had a beefsteak wrapped round their solid hearts! Nevertheless there was a heart which wanted to feel, to hear, to sing. The beefsteak was the shield to protect it from feeling too deeply, from hearing too much, from singing too sweetly. Life had to remain balanced and well-ordered.

Hamburg, too, was where Freddie had his first introduction to Shakespeare, though not at first in the city's great theatre. This theatre, where later he served his apprenticeship, had a capacity of two thousand. It was built and managed by private enterprise and its policy was modelled on Vienna's famous Burgtheater. Its first director was Viennese and so were many of the actors. The people of Hamburg took kindly to the little Vienna in their midst and the theatre flourished. During Freddie's adolescence Shakespeare was the playwright treasured above all others. All his plays were staged in sequence, in historical cycles and as Festivals.

But theatre-going was not considered necessary for children except at Christmas-time and Freddie was destined to go into business. So it was down in Hamburg's dockland that he saw his first Shakespearean play, a shortened version of *Hamlet*, roared out without the slightest inhibition by a fit-up company whose playhouse was nothing but a booth lighted with naphtha-flares, playing in one of the toughest districts of the Elbe water-front. The play had been on the boards in theatres like this one for close on two hundred years. The text was probably nearer to the *Fratricide Punished* than to Shakespeare's *Hamlet*, for it was played as a simple melodrama—all out. Their leading actor, a huge man with a voice like a kettle-drum, was also father to the family-company. He played the Ghost, making old Hamlet almost more important than young Hamlet. He thundered and roared, a flamboyant spirit, and Freddie never forgot him nor that he first heard *Hamlet* given as a dialect play, in *Plattdeutsch*, the speech of Hamburg's fishermen. Years later, in 1926, Freddie played the part himself in Berlin in Leopold Jessner's modern-dress *Hamlet*, with Fritz Kortner as the Prince of Denmark. This production was so markedly eccentric that the Ghost at first materialized dressed up as a Field-Marshal and in broad daylight—no battlements, no starlight—and later in the closet scene, he was made to rise up suddenly from the depths of a trick bed, the better to startle his unhappy son into action.

Twenty years after such wild exaggeration, and all the genuine culture that went alongside, had been swept out of existence. When Freddie went back to his hometown little remained of all he knew but the eternal river and the eternal heath lying vast and untenanted to the south-west of the ruined city. Recalling his boyhood during a sleepless night in the 1940 blitz on London, he wrote:

I want to talk about the heath of Lüneburg near Hamburg and I am going to talk quietly because that

9

was my beloved land, my country. It was a silent land
—no people in it. Some hills were swinging over it,
wide and soft like the music of a great longing. You
could come across birch-trees in youthful beauty or
juniper-bushes sinister, erect and frightening you in the
dark, when they stood like black monks. You suspected
knives in their hands.

A smell of honey was in the air on hot summer days
and I don't know where on this earth I shall ever listen
better to God's silence. Far, far away on the horizon,
across the brown land, stood black woods. There were
small paths of clean white sand, burning hot in the sun,
or suddenly pools of still dark water, a dragon-fly or
two, little brooks in green pastures. And the forests,
dark with firs or friendly with beech-trees and oaks.

I sat there and looked out over this land. In late
summer it glowed violet and red. The air vibrated and
the sand was hot.

I listened, I was restless, I didn't know what to do
with myself. I wanted to hew whole melodies out of
those hill-tops and swing them into the skies, pouring
out music into the world. Or could I write? Oh no, I
couldn't! What about taking shelter as a modest school-
master? They had long holidays, these teachers, and
could travel and dream. Would the curtain ever rise
for me, an actor behind the footlights? Yes, an actor!
Nothing more than that—but also nothing less—
burning the heart, drowning the soul in that great
ocean—the theatre.

Dreams of the past, of what has been loved, they are

good, these dreams. They shroud the bygone life in clouds of beauty and poetry. They hide the cruelty, the bitterness and the helplessness of a boyhood which did not know where to turn or how to live. I had my dreams and my despair and my doubts. How could I know that I had a talent for the acting profession? Could it not all be deadly self-delusion?

In Hamburg once more, in 1947, established master of a bi-lingual career, Freddie fell a prey to a different kind of bitterness. He could only react strenuously against everything he saw. The home where he had lived with his parents appeared to him now merely as 'an alien, dirty old house'. Watching *Romeo and Juliet* in rehearsal, from a box in his first theatre, he wrote afterwards:

My theatre. Feeling stirred a little. My theatre where I went on the stage with great awe, aged eighteen. It seemed to me at the time Olympus, a playground of the Gods who had taken on the disguise of actors. Alas, they were very average actors, very conventional, but they were honest, they believed in the theatre, they believed in art and that was all that mattered. It gave me inspiration and a clean start in my profession.

A wonderful old man helped me, Max Grube (Hamburg's theatre-director). I shall be forever thankful to him. He knew about art, he knew about talent and helped talent. He gave me an audition, alone in the foyer of the empty theatre. I presented him there with *Richard the Third*, with Franz Moor from Schiller's

Robbers and for good measure with 'Holofernes' (Hebbel). When he had sufficiently recovered he approved, he accepted me and put me straightaway into the crowd. 'No theatre-school is necessary to you,' he said, with the understanding born of long experience.

So I came to find myself in one dressing-room with all the other minor lights which went to make up the crowd in a big German theatre. I gave myself away at once; chasing across the stage with the rest of Schiller's robbers, I swung my arm so wildly that I caught another robber on the nose and laid him out cold. 'One would take you for the bandit-chief!' he cried when he came to again, outraged at such behaviour in a beginner.

In 1947 it was all drastically changed. His letter continues:

Strange declamation was going on on the stage, but the spirits—the great spirits of the great past, of great acting and producing—were absent from this shattered temple of my profession. The spirits have no medium any more to talk to the corpses in the stalls. . . . Black —black—black. It is all too much—sad and exciting, but I am happy above all that I live in England. My first impression was, pack your bag and leave this country by the next train. In Hamburg you see bad faces, without a smile and with dangerous eyes. 'Why do they stare at me?' I asked. 'Because I look Jewish?' Answer—'They don't stare at you because you look

Jewish, they stare because you look healthy and well-fed.'

Of Berlin, while wandering in and out of the Soviet Zone though officially confined to the British, Freddie wrote:

> The faces are better, the atmosphere not so oppressive, the manners are better—in short there is still the spirit of a great city of the world. . . . I shall never forget the night when I stood alone in the ruins of Hitler's Chancellery and the Berlin raindrops were falling heavily through the broken roof. . . . That is the rough outline, but heavens, what is behind the outline. . . .

In 1954, seven years later, his impression of the people of South Germany was less extreme. 'I have looked, they are not very reassuring.' Freddie had gone to Munich to play Prime Minister von Moll in a picture of the life of Richard Wagner, *Magic Fire*, with Alan Badel as Wagner. The studios were in Munich where for most of the time the actors lived. On location they were out in the country at Hohenschwangau, within sight of the Bavarian Alps, for a great part of this picture was made in and around Neuschwanstein and Hohenschwangau, the two nightmare castles of King Ludwig the Second of Bavaria. This short-lived, half-crazed monarch was Richard Wagner's patron and his plans for State Opera finance were as extravagant as his ideas on architecture, and a sore trial to Prime Minister von Moll. The remaining outdoor shots for the picture were made at the Nymphenburg Palace near Munich.

For Freddie the schedule was an easy one, less so for everyone else. Von Moll's appearances in the Wagner story were episodic though rousing, and his scenes spaced far apart. This gave Freddie a large number of free days and left him with time on his hands to study Munich, its theatres, its people, and the city itself. 'Not one talented actor on the stage,' he wrote, 'and the greatest disappointment was the direction. The audiences sit there lapping it up with great respect and patience. It is "culture". Even the onlookers who watched us filming at the Nymphenburg were overawed. The British would have grinned and released a few jokes.'

When the film-unit moved out to Hohenschwangau, Freddie had time to enjoy the mountain scenery near King Ludwig's castles and to sit by the Alpsee, a picture-book lake. . . .

There was a full moon as we drove up through the forests. The castles stood like white spectres, symbols of demented romanticism—the mentality which led the Germans direct to Nazism. But the snowclad mountains sparkled in the moonlight and a waterfall rushed down through the night. There were stars over the black pines. There one can sit on a bench and think one is a poet. It is all beautiful and lovely but I'd rather take the next plane back to London. I wondered why I was in this landscape of dreamlike beauty and delight and didn't feel at home or even at ease. Violently disturbing

14

—ghost castles. At Neuschwanstein the throne-room is in the Byzantine style but before the throne could be placed the King was dead. The concert-hall was used only once—they had concerts there in Hitler's time and the names of his singers figure on a memorial tablet—many names I knew among them.

I have gone away from Germany. I don't feel at home here any more. The people? What they say and do, it doesn't touch me. They are strangers. Strangers? I would look at strangers and at a strange country with more interest and feel more at ease.

2

THE STRATFORD ADVENTURE

The last days on the picture after the unit had returned to Munich were busy ones, as last days on a picture always are. Freddie had little time to himself, he had in any case seen all he wanted to see of the theatre in Germany. What free time he had he used for something new to him, to make the acquaintance of Bip, for the great mime, Marcel Marceau, was in Munich during his second tour of Western Germany. Freddie flew back to London immediately after that, his part in *Magic Fire* completed. He could talk of nothing but Marceau and Bip, walking against the wind, and the boy with the butterfly—here, at last, was genius, here was supremacy in its own chosen field. The immediate must, for all of us, was to see Marceau—'But will Marceau bring Bip to London?' 'If not—we go to him.'

On the German theatre the sorry verdict was that Hitler had done his work as thoroughly and destructively as Oliver Cromwell had done in England when he closed the theatres, and a decade of acting experience was lost beyond recall. Any direct link with the style of acting known to Shakespeare was broken then, except that Hitler had achieved the same effect without closing the theatres.

Freddie had seen every show he could get to while he

was away. As he sat and analysed each and every one of them it was easy to see that he was tired of film-work, eager for another play. His last stage role had been in the spring, when he played Marcus Hoff in *The Big Knife*. This had followed two years of film-work. Before that, in 1952, he had appeared as the father in Yvonne Mitchell's *The Same Sky*, with Canada's Frances Hyland playing his elder daughter. No Shakespeare parts had come along in four years, since he last played Shylock at the Glasgow Citizens' Theatre, with Douglas Campbell, and on Shakespeare Freddie had been trained. Movies were excellent business, said Freddie, but he would like to make 1955 a theatre year and he would like to play Shakespeare, yet here we were in November already and not a sign of any play upon the horizon.

It was a wet afternoon on this November day. Our two sons had a holiday from school and time hung heavy on their hands. 'Now, we all go out and learn how they play theatre in Canada,' said their father, hailing a taxi from the doorstep as the rain beat down on us. He swept us all off to the Marble Arch Pavilion to see *The Stratford Adventure*, which was showing there with the latest Italian movie, and that was the real beginning of our own adventure in Stratford, Ontario.

We came into the middle of a continuous programme at the end of the Italian movie, sat through the newsreel and then there, shining in the sun, paddled the Stratford swans. There was the river Avon, the willows, and the island bridge, and behind all this, dominating a quiet meadow and backed by trees, stood the Tent Theatre.

Summer in Ontario and not only summer, the Festival also was in bloom.

As the swans sailed by, two tall figures, Dr and Mrs Guthrie, walked down the aisle of the cinema and settled peacefully in two empty seats exactly in front of those we had chosen for ourselves. Their presence at this showing of the Stratford picture was, as we later found, as unpremeditated as our own. While the story of Stratford, Ontario, unfolded, from the birth of an idea, through the hazards of putting it into action, until the actual performances in the First Stratford Shakespearean Festival, we watched, over the Festival Director's shoulder, his face and person on the screen, together with all those others which, a few months later, were to become the faces of friends.

We saw inside the Tent for the first time, looking in wonder at the action of the fastest *Richard III* ever seen. Freddie drew in his breath and sat forward in his seat. He had many a time had a crack at Richard III himself and he never tired of seeing other actors in his favourite roles. Richard Crookback had been the man to get Freddie into the theatre, Richard had been his first Shakespearean star-part in his first season as leading actor in Lübeck, at the age of twenty-four. That was a long time ago but, like so many actors who portray this extraordinary king, he had a great affection for the man.

Now we sat watching Alec Guinness, marvellously dressed, on a stage whose mechanics were entirely new. Richard III struggled with his destiny, phantoms paraded, armies engaged and the crisis of the play approached.

18

The action keyed up, swords flashed and glittered. Robin and William were already deep in a heraldic phase; some-one had given them a book full of pictures of knights in armour, brightly coloured for ages five and seven, and to-day they were in ecstasy. 'That's a good battle!' breathed the voice of the expert straight into the coat-collar of the man who had directed the battle. Happily it was a small voice not loud enough on this occasion to disturb.

When the lights went up and the picture was over far too soon, and our sons went, famished, to stock up with ice-cream after the recent excitement, there was a short lull, grown-up eye caught grown-up eye with the surprise of recognition. There was news to be exchanged, a great Director to be congratulated—that was that and we went home. It was dark by this time, street-lights glittered on the wet pavements and when supper was over and the children in bed, we talked for a long time of new ways in the theatre, the speed and vitality of the action at Stratford and the scope the great arena gave to actors and director alike. Freddie explored the subject from voice-production to crowd movements, taking the pulse of this new life infused into ancient ritual. *The Stratford Adventure* was a first-class documentary, vivid but challenging, with its Tent so like a Greek theatre, yet so unlike—tantalizing also, being twice as far away.

Two days later: 'There's Dr Guthrie on the phone.' Our cleaner spoke with the special voice reserved for illness or accident—not your usual doctor either, her tone im-plied '. . . must speak to Freddie, tell him I have a plan,'

19

said the well-known voice at the end of the wire. We had lunch the same day with the Guthries at their home in Lincoln's Inn Fields, looking out upon the plane trees. 'Come out to Canada and play Shylock'—there it was, quite simply—'bring the family.' So the future of 1955 was settled for us in a matter of minutes. It was to be a theatre year. It was to be Shakespeare.

On our way home from lunch we bought a new copy of *The Merchant of Venice* and Shylock came out of the deep-freeze. A huge fresh horizon had opened for us, a marvel of a theatre at the end of an immense journey. We both had severe travel fever immediately and Freddie the actor was caught by the opportunities of an arena stage, both technical and artistic. He had never before played on a similar stage nor in a theatre-festival since he appeared as Banquo, and also as Peter Quince in *A Midsummer Night's Dream* at Heidelberg. He had enjoyed that Festival played in the open air, using the great façade of Heidelberg Castle for a backdrop. Later he had been cast for Oberon in another production of *The Dream*, for which role he would normally have been considered too heavy. Accordingly he played the part not as an irritable fairy but as an angry forest demon, as unconventional as it was successful—and now, what would the Stratford Tent do for his Shylock? For here was as unconventional a theatre as any man could wish for and some kind of drastic revaluation there would have to be.

The Shylock Freddie played in Germany he had developed at the German theatre in Prague. In Britain during the early years of the war, Tyrone Guthrie, then in command at the Old Vic's headquarters in Burnley, cast Freddie as Shylock in his first Shakespearean part on the English stage, thereby releasing him from the greatest hardship of his emigration. Mr Guthrie did not on this occasion direct the play himself. The tour of the play covered mines, schools, and army camps and playing Shylock in English was enough for Freddie at this time, without re-reading the character as well.

Any attempt to adapt this Shylock for the arena stage was not going to be of the slightest use, he must be made new altogether. As an actor Freddie had never agreed with nor conformed to the practice, so long kept alive in Germany, of presenting Shylock as a buffoon-cum-scapegoat; his Shylock had at all times been enlarged from life. He was accustomed to big theatres—European playhouses are in general much bigger than British ones—but an amphitheatre seating two thousand appears far larger to the actors than a theatre with several balconies and the same capacity. If the values of the arena stage were going to be so different from anything he had met before, so must the characterization be. For long hours he brooded in his room or went for walks all over London. In the evenings we worked at the language. There was as yet little sign of the new Shylock, but he was stirring none the less.

Christmas came and passed and in the New Year the first job of 1955 was again a movie, *I am a Camera*, in which Freddie played the doctor.

Towards the end of January a cloud was blown on to our cloudless horizon, from a quarter quite unexpected by ourselves. We learnt from Montreal that certain elements in the New World considered *The Merchant of Venice* to be an anti-Semitic play. We had been used to thinking of it as a plea for Jewry—no matter, it is now common knowledge that there was such a controversy and some opposition to any production of *The Merchant* at Stratford, Ontario, also that many a worthier subject has been less well aired. Sitting at home in Britain we remembered the coal-miner who gripped Freddie's hand after a show on that Old Vic tour, exclaiming, 'Why didn't you get your pound of flesh?' with a fervour not wholly due to meat-rationing, and the miner's wife who murmured, 'I felt so sorry for Shylock.' We hoped the rumour from Canada was untrue.

There had been a young airman, too, in a camp near Derby, who had inquired at the box-office if 'The Merchant of Venison' was the big picture. And the eccentric most dear to memory, the Polish Colonel, one among thousands of the Polish Air Force stationed in Perth during World War II. Freddie took it for granted that the Poles would be hostile to the last man to Shylock and perhaps himself, but they filled the theatre to the last seat and they were an exemplary audience. After the show the Colonel found his way backstage, to the communal dressing-room, where he made a lengthy speech addressed to Freddie entirely in Polish. Freddie, expecting at the least a challenge to a duel, understood not one word, but the gist was clearly not in that direction. The speech ended surprisingly, with a kiss delivered Russian-style, and the Pole went on his way.

These and some others we remembered almost as people

in a story, but there had also been the young woman on a bus in Glasgow. She had tapped, or rather struck Freddie heavily on the shoulder from the seat behind his own. Very much startled, he looked round into the face of a sleeping baby, wrapped together with its mother in a shawl.

'You,' said the baby's mother, 'were you the Jew?'

Guardedly he answered, 'Yes.' Not being long out of Europe, he wondered what was coming next.

'Good,' said the woman and she said nothing more, only sat and crooned quietly to her baby.

Remembering all this and that Freddie had played Shylock in Germany and Czechoslovakia without incident and all over the British Isles, where there were fifty thousand refugees from Hitler, without a single protest, we decided the rumour must be unfounded. At best it had a musty flavour, it must be artificial. Another trip to Europe swept it from our minds.

Though the months ahead of us were fully planned, the journey into the past was by no means over yet. Freddie was playing with the idea of a flying visit to Prague. Negotiations with South German Radio were complete for some work he was to do in connexion with the Schiller Celebrations of the coming year, but there were a few weeks to go before he was needed at the radio-station in Stuttgart and now seemed the time for Prague. He had never revisited Czechoslovakia after he left Prague sixteen days before the Nazi tanks rolled in. He had loved Prague like no other place he knew, a city basking in an autumnal heyday of the arts before the Hitler-blight fell on it.

In the free democracy of Czechoslovakia, life before World War II was pleasant, sunny, and expansive. Prague shone from the heights above the river Moldau streaming down through the Bohemian plateau to join the Elbe. Beyond the city stretched the forests and rich farmlands of Bohemia and beneath the soil lay great mineral wealth. Czech, Slovak, Moravian, and German population-groups lived side by side with comparatively little friction, for their country was more than a free democracy, it was a tolerant and a liberal one. As such it attracted, and especially to Prague, some of the best minds among the refugees from the Hitler-terror now convulsing Germany. Most of them were Jewish and a very large proportion of them artists. In return for their freedom and the right to live, they enriched Prague with their personalities and the varied fruits of their work and formed a colony of their own, unlike any other at that time in Europe. The unique astringent humour of the easy-going Czech formed a matrix round them, bracing the Jew and saving the German from over-intensity. Freddie joined them at the request of a former Director in Hamburg, now established at the German theatre in Prague. Among them he was happy and Prague saw some of his best roles. The theatre-life, together with the other artists, formed a society of its own, not consciously aloof from the world of industry, commerce, and banking from which the audiences of the German theatre were drawn, but separate from the lives of their patrons, sunk, of set purpose, into the work in hand, for well they knew their peace would not be lasting.

24

Across the border, Germany seethed. It was only necessary to switch on the radio to hear Hitler barking. Rumours there were, that he would bark himself to death, but none dared hope for this, and there was work to be done, while still there was time to do it and the lovely country of their refuge to enjoy. But it was an enclosed country they had come to, offering little in the way of escape in time of danger; aircraft only for millionaires, no outlet to the sea, one navigable river running straight into Hitler's territory, and the railroad to the Baltic must cross Poland before reaching Gdynia nearly four hundred miles to the north. Hitler was after the Skoda munition-works, Czech industry, and any radio-active deposits he could lay his hands on. He was determined to have Czechoslovakia at any price and without going to war he took it. On many of his victims he inflicted a devastation worse than war. If he did not have their lives he took their faith in their fellow-men and in such a way as made it hard, or impossible, to recover. Before invading a country he destroyed from within. Every walk of life came to know his agents, adept at spreading rumour or sowing strife, expert in forgery, bribery, and undercover intimidation of the weak. If unable to tap the telephone, they steamed open letters; failing either diversion elaborate case-sheets were prepared, listing iniquities such as being, as Freddie was, president of an actors' club. Their efforts sometimes collapsed into sheer farce, as on the day when Freddie borrowed an egg from a friend for his breakfast. Practical jokes were not unknown in Prague and, wishing to repay the kindness, Freddie decided, later in the morning, to return another egg, fried nice and thin, on a greased paper slipped beneath a badly fitting door. The owner of the flat was out and did not return immediately, but the local spy, who had been watching Freddie, fished out his offering from under the door, believing it to be a secret message. How he decoded a congealed fried egg was never known, but he himself could, from then on, be identified.

Only very seldom could things work out harmlessly like this. Hitler was on the threshold. Anxiety and terror mounted in the German-Jewish refugees. Freddie's own plans ranged from taking a football team to the Argentine to learning shoe-making. He had been gravely ill in the summer of 1938, with scarlet-fever followed at once by diphtheria, and was not fully recovered. Came the Munich crisis and painters, poets, actors, writers scattered to the four corners of the earth as the direct and immediate result. They were genuine fugitives, peaceful, harmless, creative people, the very last that any adult civilization can afford to do without. Many of them were now on the run for the second time, taking with them their one transportable asset, their creative power. Down came the curtain on the German theatre in Prague. The first rehearsal of *Hamlet* with Freddie as King Claudius had just taken place when the theatre closed its doors on a German-speaking company. Thereafter the Czechs would have none of them. They could never work again in Czechoslovakia and Germany was closed to them.

Freddie, returning to the theatre after his long illness, was convinced that his attack of diphtheria had ruined his voice for life. With that on his mind began the first period of unemployment he had ever known, and this, though he had no inkling at the time, allowed his damaged vocal cords to heal completely and ultimately saved his voice for his English-speaking career. Workless in Prague, he went as far as planning a visit to France. He took a few desultory English lessons, but though he knew the noose which Hitler would throw round Czechoslovakia must fall round his neck also, the inertia of despair so weighed him down that during the long autumn of 1938 he made no move and came to no decision.

During the weeks before the Munich crisis, trusted colleagues from the German theatre mysteriously vanished, Nazi agents every one of them. They rode back into Prague on the armoured vehicles when Hitler took over early in March 1939; no longer humble actors and stage-hands, Gestapo-men now in jack-boots, holding every card from blackmail to deportation. But they were too late for Freddie. When the Gestapo came searching for him, his name high on their wanted list, he had just left Czechoslovakia. He could not avoid the mental suffering of the refugee but the physical horrors were spared him, nor did he have to flee in panic and disorder on the historic train which was held for the sake of last-minute fugitives, with steam up in Prague station, until the Nazi tanks lumbered on to the platforms. The train pulled out then, before the tanks could open fire, and beat the Nazis to the Polish border, later to deliver many hundred passengers in safety to Gdynia.

Freddie arranged things otherwise. It was years since

he had lived in his homeland. No one would expect to find him there, so he crossed Germany by rail, quietly and without fuss, en route for Britain, and such was the inefficiency of the Nazi machine, he met with courtesy and friendliness all the way.

On the journey to Britain to be an actor—at first without a language to work with, at first a man without a permit to work—in the fresh bitterness of exile he put his feeling on a scrap of paper:

Prague—the theatre, when the curtain rises won't they sense me, those people in Prague? Won't they think—now is his entrance? They must feel that I am present in their theatre—Surely! I live in the curtain, in those dark red stalls, in the orchestra-pit where they tune their instruments—I smell grease-paint in the dressing-rooms. The hairdressers rattle their curling-tongs. I watch the gallery filling up and I look down into the bright cave of the theatre. Friends are coming in and suddenly I smell good coffee, they prepare it for the interval. More and more people are coming in. Excitement is humming—joy. Friends! Don't you know? Here I am—here!

This mood passed but Prague remained in Freddie's mind,

the most beautiful city I know. A gorgeous cloudburst of baroque with the sharp edge of Gothic. Impossible to walk quickly through these streets while miracles

Shylock. The Old Vic, 1941

Mephistopheles

Wozzek

smiled at every step and every spirit who ever lived between Výsehrad hill and the Hradzin palace was still on his feet weaving the music of Prague's golden saga of the millenniums. . . .

After the war Czechoslovakia had been off the map altogether with the rest of the Soviet satellite states. When the curtain went up again in Prague, the Iron Curtain came down. No former citizen could visit the Iron Curtain countries from the West with any reasonable certainty of coming back. In the last year, however, things had eased and Freddie's plans to spend a week in Prague were almost complete when another part in a picture, *Case for Murder*, came up, on location in Berlin this time. So instead of flying to the Bohemian capital he took a plane to snowbound Berlin. He liked it no better than he had a few years earlier, writing, 'I don't like Berlin with its face pushed in. I don't like the air of apologetic hopelessness. What can you expect of people living in a rubble-heap? Theatre? The juice is lacking and the spark and the great director too. . . .' 'A skeleton,' he said briefly on his return, 'with make-up.'

In March followed a flight to Stuttgart to make a pre-recording of *The Wallenstein Trilogy* for the Schiller Centenary in May 1955. Freddie played one of the favourite roles of his life, the General, Wallenstein, directed by Leopold Lindtberg. The date of the broadcast was the day that we were scheduled to arrive in Canada. Writing from the radio-station, between scenes, he said, 'There is nothing to record but work and of course my style does not fit at once with modern German acting . . .' and on a free day towards the end of the time:

I shall use this day for a little journey into the past— by train through the Neckar valley to Heidelberg, change trains and travel to Darmstadt. Maybe I take a walk through the town and back to work to-morrow. So, with Berlin and Hamburg the journey into the past is complete.

From Monday I shall prepare for Canada. About Canada I am sure. We will travel with light and happy hearts. . . .

3

SPRINGBOARD

On the Monday following the plane from Stuttgart was eight hours late coming in. London Airport would give no reason for the delay till half an hour before the touch-down. Aircraft flew in from India, Rome, New York, and Montreal, every one of them on time. But the reason was simple enough, the Stuttgart plane had been delayed by fog; every part of Germany was deep in fog and Berlin Airport closed. Out of the fog came Freddie. A mountain of letters awaited him at home, some of them from Stratford, Ontario. With a kind of finality he unpacked his things and put them away. The journey into the past was over, he said, and attacked his Stratford mail. Out fell a Festival Programme and, like a trick in time, the past had gone ahead of us to come up untarnished and vital in Canada, a land where the terrible habits of Central Europe were happily unknown. In addition to a third season of Shakespearean drama, Marcel Marceau, whom Freddie had so lately seen in Munich, was to present his Bip at the first Stratford Musical Festival; that we knew, but here he was, appearing in the Musical Festival as the Devil in *A Soldier's Tale* as well. This devil was an old acquaintance, not quite as domesticated as the Mephis-topheles of Goethe's *Faust*. Freddie himself had never played him but he had taken the Narrator's part in *A Soldier's Tale* in Berlin and again in Prague, where it formed part of a double bill with George Büchner's soldier drama *Wozzek*. Over and above this, the whole of the drama programme, *Oedipus Rex* and *Julius Caesar*, had a living interest almost as great as *The Merchant*.

The town of Darmstadt, revisited only a week ago, had first given Freddie the part of King Oedipus. The tragedy was acted, not in masks, in the lovely old playhouse built originally as a court theatre, private to the Dukes of Hesse, their relatives, courtiers and hangers-on. Freddie had been cast as Oedipus again in Prague, this time in modern dress, and in Prague a few months before his first sally as Othello he played Caesar.

During the last weeks in Germany, what had become of the preparations for Canada? What had happened to Shylock during the journey into the past? Memories of him must have been revived, for Shylock had the longest case-history for Freddie of all his parts except perhaps Mephistopheles, who had followed him round in his theatre life, almost after the manner of a familiar spirit in a Renaissance story.

Freddie had originally walked on in *The Merchant* in the Hamburg theatre's crowd. It may truthfully be said that he came out of the First World War to go into *The Merchant of Venice*. A conscript in the Kaiser's army, he described himself as 'an unhappy warrior—the best day of my military life was the day I discarded my uniform'. So as to do this in the shortest possible time after the debacle of the German forces in 1918, among many others Freddie demobilized himself. In Hamburg the theatre was short of actors and he was eager to get back to work and home. Army life was as tedious as it was brutal and he had learnt all the parts he had been able to take with him to the war, among them Iago, Malvolio and Oedipus Rex. He was for some time billeted in a farmhouse at Le Cateau in Northern France with a family who became his lifelong friends. In these tranquil surroundings he learnt French while the guns grumbled in the distance. He was encouraged to study for his profession and spent many happy hours sitting under a peach tree learning Shakespeare. But with the signing of the Armistice and Kaiser Wilhelm's abdication and flight a sad restlessness attacked his stranded armies. The majority dourly waited for the order to demobilize, but not Freddie and a handful of young and hopeful friends. In a mood midway between Candide and the Good Soldier Schweik they commandeered a truck and set off home across the ruined countryside of Northern France. They repatriated three Belgian refugees they had befriended on the way and when their truck at last ran out of petrol they were lucky enough to find a railway still capable of running trains and a train bound for Germany. Freddie walked into the family home in Hamburg unannounced, bringing with him a sizeable roast, obtained by barter on the way, to please his mother. He discarded the uniform which irked him so and was back in the theatre the same day. That evening's play was *The Merchant of Venice*, with one of his most admired actors, Julius Kobler, as Shylock.

Freddie did not play Shylock himself for five or six years. He had first to graduate from supporting parts in

Hamburg's great theatre to major roles in a smaller play-house in Lübeck, one hour by rail from Hamburg. He loved Lübeck and went back there again and again as guest artist, arrogant, self-contained, and almost medieval though the city might be. It was known as the City of Seven Churches in deference to the gigantic brick buildings whose high walls and copper roofs and spires sailed above the ancient ramparts like ships upon a plain.

Here also the people loved beefsteaks and mature red wine. They took their new young leading actor to their hearts and affectionately named him 'King of Lübeck'. He played heavy leads and character parts, warriors, tyrants, villains and old men: Mephistopheles in Marlowe's *Doctor Faustus*, Richard III, Death in *Everyman*. No romantic leads ever came his way—Tybalt, never Romeo. Something in him struggled for an outlet in comedy, as the Press notices of that date amply bear out. But no such outlet was offered him at this time, except for an occasional frolic in a part like Ferrovius in Bernard Shaw's *Androcles and the Lion*, or Professor Higgins in *Pygmalion*. The combination of his warm humanity with a great leaning towards the funny side of life, and towards its expression in comedy, was overlooked. Voice, build and colouring all weighed against its expression in the theatre. What was wanted of Freddie was to be sombre, statuesque, dæmonic or horrifying. Though he occasionally relaxed with parts like Harry Hotspur and Pistol (*Henry IV*), Tubal or Petruc-chio, in the main he was kept to the heaviest of starring parts, often in the gloomiest of plays. Apart from Shylock, two roles especially followed him from theatre to theatre—

34

Mephistopheles and Napoleon. Failing them, Ibsen or Strindberg would be in the bill with parts like John Gabriel Borkman, Masterbuilder Solness or the Captain in *The Dance of Death*, and German tragedy rang the changes with Shakespeare. Magnificent training for an actor, but so unremitting that Freddie himself grew to feel that it eventually impeded by its very monotony, and went far towards halting development during his middle years.

The first attack on Shylock came in Darmstadt—a lonely Shylock, so the critics reckoned—standing up like a crag and played in complete isolation from the other characters in the play. Not long after that Freddie was cast as Tubal, a part he treasured as a super-Shylock, in a star-studded production of *The Merchant* in Berlin, with Elisabeth Bergner as Portia and Fritz Kortner playing Shylock.

Prague saw another version of *The Merchant* less ambitious than Berlin's and Freddie's Shylock was here described as a man without music—not the plaything of destiny but its underwriter. He had perhaps something of the pathos of the Golem but more of the Golem's master.

Shylock in Northern England inherited from all his predecessors, not forgetting Tubal, yet he had an austerity of character, as in dress, which belonged to the working conditions of the tours and which, on Stratford's arena-stage, would look like a line-drawing done where a sculpture was commissioned. 'Shakespeare at the Coal-face' was one name for these tours and this war-time Shylock was pictured as a farouche, retiring man, He had a touch of the religious fanatic as he stalked black-robed across the narrow stages of miners' halls and community centres. He was

neither extravagant nor ostentatious, a rich man prefer-
ring not to seem so lest he inflame the envy of his fellow-
Venetians, the Gentiles of whom he was suspicious from
the rise of the curtain. At the Citizens' Theatre in Glasgow
the differences were superficial; basically it was the same
reading of the part, unbending, just and ruthless, passion-
ate only towards his child.

None of this was now sufficient. None of this was suited
to a Festival. This characterization was too domestic, too
precise and too detached except during the Passion Scene.
Freddie's thoughts roamed back and forth—the Golem?
That variation had not satisfied him before, it had been an
idea hinged on to the Prague legend, of interest only to
audiences in Prague. If there was anything of the Golem
among Shakespeare's creations it would, in any event, be-
long of right to Caliban. Freddie's visit to Heidelberg a
week previously had set his mind working again around
A Midsummer Night's Dream and focused his ideas once more
upon Oberon. If, he said, he could have played his Oberon
in the Heidelberg setting, he would have given him twice
as much punch as was possible on the proscenium stage.
What if Oberon, so often no more than petulant, were to
break into *The Dream* like a walking tree in a glade of rose-
bushes? What if Oberon, instead of pleading, threatened,
gigantic and ominous while moonlight bleached the façade
of Heidelberg Castle? Picture something on those lines—it
was perfectly feasible, given the chance he would have
done it—the Stratford Tent could and must bring about
the same kind of liberation for Shylock.

So much for the idea of the hornet in fairyland. Whether

it was the lapse of years or whether it was that some of the sunshine we had seen in *The Stratford Adventure* had already seeped through into ourselves, we could not say, but when it came to our evening work upon the part, much of the initial savagery and bitterness had drained out of Shylock. As the weeks passed he became far less of a man with a grievance; certainly he was not a jolly Jew but he had become a genial one, at least during the opening passages of the play.

The evenings were devoted to *The Merchant* but the days were busy enough. 'You are blessed of God!' a hurried Italian waitress in a Soho restaurant had once exclaimed, flinging down two plates of spaghetti in front of us, sitting too astonished to reply. She was gone before we could thank her for her unusual greeting. Perhaps it had something to do with our new son, Robin, left at home today while we ate out? The restaurant was not a smart one and we had ventured to tell this waitress, as she flew by for the tenth time, that the baby would be waiting far from silently for his lunch at home, if we delayed much longer in Soho. Back she came now, harassed yet serene, carrying a little silver bowl of cheese, grated to the consistency of large specks of dust. She spooned out the cheese liberally upon our plates. 'Those who have the *bambini* are blessed of God. Those who have not the *bambini* do not know what they miss!' She was off again, doling out meals at a distant table. She had made her simple statement and did not wish to elaborate; it was obvious she knew what she was talking about. With the passage of time the 'blessings of

God' had grown large and lively; London was often a tight fit for them and these two children needed to spend more of their growing time than school holidays allowed outside a town so big. Our trip to Canada gave us the opportunity, undreamed of in most families in Britain or anywhere else, to travel them with their father's job and show them the world at an early age. There was no knowing where they might work and live when they were old enough to choose for themselves and they were old enough now, though only just, to remember all the essentials of the trip.

In the museum area of South Kensington, ten minutes from our home, there are not only daily film-shows, documentaries from all parts of the Commonwealth, there is also a map of Canada the size of a wall in any ordinary room. It is brightly coloured, showing Canada's natural resources, and has the added fascination of being worked by twelve electric buttons easy enough for the hands of a five-year-old to manipulate. Press one button and the uranium lights up, press others and you get an idea of the forests, the grain-belt or the fruit-farms of Ontario. There we stood the little boys and let them push the buttons to their hearts' content. They had outgrown infant school as peas outgrow a pod, so for the few weeks left before we sailed we packed them off to Devonshire to spend April in an old stone manor-house from whose garden ploughed fields of dark red earth rolled down towards the sea. Primroses flowered under the hedges and the only traffic which held up the cows, moving slowly home at milking-time, consisted of large families of sedate farm ducks waddling across the narrow lanes. Soon we should see how the little boys adapted themselves to a deep-water passage and to the manner of life across the Atlantic.

In London came the tenants, the prospective tenants to examine our house. We led them to the top of the stairs and led them down again. Mostly that was all. 'Those stairs!' They all said it, when they had recovered breath, with reproach in their voices. 'But no basement,' we retaliated, yet they were not so easily won by the tower-like, narrow house-plan so attractive to London's speculative builders about a hundred years ago. One afternoon not long before we sailed for Canada, we came in to find a mysterious name written on the telephone-pad. The owner of the name had an order to view the house and the hour was now. Time to call up the letting-agency? 'A Siamese diplomat,' we were hurriedly told, a prince, they believed, and a married man. Our door-bell rang. There stood the Siamese diplomat smiling like a seraph and clinging to his arm was his exquisite wife, also smiling. They could speak almost no English and we no word of Siamese. They were from the East where probably they lived in palaces made of marble lace with turquoise floors and fountains everywhere. They were both very small, very decorative and looked extremely fragile. From the outset the attempts at conversation were farcical, proceeding almost completely at cross-purposes. Smiles were the mainstay of the interview. The Siamese looked carefully at everything and finally bowed themselves gracefully off our doorstep, saying diplomatically that perhaps and probably they would rent the house. We expressed our delight, we were sorry to see them go because they were so beautiful, but we were

not surprised on our arrival at Stratford to hear that our
tenants were Scottish, immune to staircases, and had quite
another name.

Soon we were in the first days of May. Rehearsals for
the Festival were already beginning in Stratford, Ontario.
We said our goodbyes and left London without incident
other than Robin's sixth birthday celebrations. Expect-
ancy mingled with relief when at last the sailing-date came.
The steamship company from now on was right behind us,
until we landed in Canada. Provided we had sense enough
to board the boat-train the steamship company undertook
to deliver us, as we innocently supposed, at the appointed
day and hour in Montreal. We called up the taxi-rank and
simultaneously Grock, a new and indispensable toy dog,
lost a brown glass eye. It had not been fixed to stand the
strain of hitting the ceiling. Impossible to travel with a
one-eyed dog. The Cyclops, we pleaded, had only one eye
but that information was brushed aside. Out of the question to set foot on the boat without the eye, and the eye
could not be found. It had lodged on the top of a high
shelf and was not located till our return to London—meanwhile impossible to sail for Canada, said the sturdy owner
planted desperately in the middle of the carpet. A new-
looking but infinitely small taxi pulled up at the door.
Happily the driver was a slow-moving man and a piece
of simple surgery involving a rug-needle and two pink
pearl buttons could be carried out upon the dog. He became an albino but what matter? our exit from the country
was no longer barred though time was passing.

Silently, almost as if it had not meant to go at all, the

boat-train pulled out of Euston Station and we were on our way to Liverpool. North London slid away behind us, rank upon rank of grey houses. Soon we were out in the open country where great heavy spires of blossom on the chestnut trees were almost over and the apple and pear trees and the lilacs in full bloom in people's gardens. Grazing cows looked like cardboard cut-outs from the windows of the moving train. The meadows were green as we trundled through the Midlands, the corn well up, lambs fat and woolly. England already had a look of summer.

Our train came to a standstill within a few feet of the boat—Liverpool is not as haphazard as it looks. Time to give our farewell postcards to an Irish porter and board the boat. The sunshine, so friendly on the train journey, deserted us now and we dropped down the Mersey in a raw white mist and could see nothing of the country we were leaving behind us.

The sea passage was uneventful, a resting phase between two geographical extremes. We had sailed away from a group of islands with a very small, thickly populated land surface and a coastline which, taken all together, would stretch from Liverpool to Vancouver, and we were making for a country so vast that it contained, we had been told, a million lakes and had living space for more than a hundred million people.

Grey wastes of gently heaving water soon palled upon our children though not on us. The marvel of travelling so fast while still there was no sight of land went on too long, the North Atlantic was too unfurnished for a small boy's taste. No other ships were to be seen upon this run and no icebergs—Henry Hudson was the current hero and he had done wonders with icebergs—and they grieved over the lack of whales. They kept watch but there were neither whales nor icebergs on this trip, only the gulls trailed our ship across the ocean, diving into her wake for titbits. At what invisible and undefended frontier the North American gulls took over from the Europeans we could not guess, perhaps they were all from a Greenland patrol; and to our sons' insistent demands that the ship should be re-routed via Hudson Bay we could only reply that we had not come out to seek the North-West Passage, nor was a visit to Hudson Bay planned for this trip. The boat was bound for Montreal on what was beginning to look like a tight schedule.

PART 2

CANADA

The Tent Theatre, Stratford, Ontario

Doctor Kurtz in *Thunder Rock*. London, 1940

4

LAND OF THE FUTURE

Off Newfoundland, on the fourth day out, we saw the first gannet, solitary, white and aloof, circling over the water in wide sweeps, hardly moving her wings. She was operating far more leisurely than her cousins in the Hebrides, who drop like dive-bombers from a hundred feet out of a clear sky and rise dripping from the green water, gulping herrings. This one continued circling with a kind of be-spectacled seriousness but she did not seem to catch any fish. That she was there at all meant Cape Race must be less than eighty miles away, not that we were likely to see it. The early morning sky was leaden and looked as if threatening a heavy snowfall. The snow held off but from one minute to the next our ship drove into a dense, icy fog-blanket. There she dawdled, fog-horns braying.

Passengers at breakfast were at first only dimly aware of the state of the weather, talk centred round today's movie-show. The big picture listed on the programme was a more recent one than had yet been shown on this voyage, a British picture, *The Colditz Story*. Freddie played a feature part in it, the German Commandant of Colditz prison-fortress, with his hair clipped to the limit and a genuine Hitler Iron Cross complete with swastika. His real-life counterpart at Colditz Castle had taken care of many of

45   E

Germany's most priceless art treasures along with the escape-men and he had been so much liked by his prisoners that it was said he was invited along with all of them to attend the premiere of the picture in London.

Sitting drinking his breakfast coffee, Freddie was pressed for his verdict on this picture. Publicity stills on the ship's board concentrated only on the stars. Thoughtfully he ran his hand over his now well-grown hair and we remembered the horrified glances of quiet-living people at the seaside where we were on vacation at the time his part was being shot. Again he was asked: was *Colditz* a horror-picture? 'No, no,' he answered without irony, 'it is history, my sons will see it,' and mildly added as an afterthought, perhaps the questioner had better see it too and make sure of the quality.

Late-comers to breakfast brought with them a ship's rumour—several hours late already on her time schedule. Our gannet should still have been roosting on a distant rock, when we steamed past the point where we saw her fishing. Fog was even thicker up above and if it lasted any time at all the schedule would be disrupted altogether. We went on deck where we could hardly see the rail; here we were imprisoned in the fog, feeling like the men in Colditz. But a few hours' delay getting into Montreal might give us a chance to hear the 'Wallenstein' broadcast from South-German Radio, supposing the wireless operator was willing and able to pick it up; then came the first of many calculations of East-West Atlantic time. But no, Freddie was no longer intent on 'Wallenstein'. Shakespeare had ousted Schiller and in good earnest he began to fret about

46

being late for his first rehearsal of *The Merchant of Venice*. Impossible to be late for rehearsal, it didn't bear contemplating, it would be an affront to the theatre. Nothing, nothing whatever must interfere with rehearsals. There was a Festival ahead for which every performance must be ready and perfect. No matter what the weather might do, we had to be in Stratford on time. He went up the companionway leading to the boat-deck and became invisible, incubating Shylock in the fog. Above his head the fog-horns bleated, our vessel barely moved, and the long swell of a following sea travelled faster than we did.

'Mr Frederick Valk, Mr Frederick Valk.' Through the mists and coughing slightly came a ship's messenger with a radio-telegram. Driven below for warmth we read the first message from the Stratford Festival's publicity department. It broke the news of a combined welcoming party and Press reception awaiting us in Montreal at seven-thirty in the evening of the day we were supposed to dock and requested our presence there. The purser was consulted on the quiet, but he would only say, after the guarded manner of his kind, 'You won't get ashore at all till the day after. Lucky if we dock before the next morning.' He sounded very pleased about it. Till his unwelcome forecast should be known about the ship, best keep it quiet. Then the second telegram arrived directing us to leave the boat to its fate—it said 'ship delayed' and suggested we disembark at Quebec City, where a taxi would meet and drive us to Montreal.

Quebec to Montreal, with a glimpse of French Canada on the way, it was a wonderful idea. The little boys had

had enough of the boat and were ready to disembark there and then, for beaver-life had ousted Henry Hudson. But Quebec to Montreal? London to Liverpool, as the crow flies the distances must be much the same—it seemed a long way for a taxi. Approached again, the purser was more cheerful. Fog notwithstanding, the ship would tie up at Quebec early on the day of the Montreal party. We could guess at no reason for such sudden optimism, considering the woolly blanket that still wrapped the ship, but in the event the purser was right. Recollections came of London taxis, grindingly leisured, tiny as matchboxes, with all but the lightest hand-baggage slung from a strap near the driver. We radioed Stratford, Ontario, hardly liking to, fearing to be exacting, and hinted at a large taxi. This effort caused some merriment in the Festival offices, while the ship nosed her way towards the Gulf and we sat warm in the cinema and amazed our sons with their father's monocled and military presence at Colditz Castle.

Some fifty miles east of Anticosti the fog lifted and the ship began to move. Vibrating till her plates creaked, she cut through the water and we had not long been travelling at this pace before a small, brown, speckled landbird met the ship and settled on one of the rails. The sea passage was over. We had entered the mouth of the St Lawrence and the journey up-river to Quebec is one which those who make it for the first time will never forget. The bird flew off and we put ourselves under the wing of a French-Canadian couple returning home from a visit to France. Most of the remaining hours of this trip were spent with them, standing on the shelter-deck below where the little

48

bird had perched and hearing of the husband's boyhood
on the Isle de Bic some fifty years ago, and how later he
had left the island with his wife to take over a logging concern nearer Montreal. Steaming past Gaspé our new
friends told us how the Vikings who had colonized Britain's Western Isles, from the Orkneys to the Isle of Man,
were thought to have been there too. We wondered how
long it had taken them to cross the ocean and what the
Indians had made of the 'pirate swarm out of the northern
hive', as one Manx song describes them. They occupied
our islands on the principle of grab and sail away, leaving
our primitive Celtic civilization destroyed. Perhaps the
Canadian Indian tribes had had better luck with them.

Looking across towards the Seven Islands, we watched
the coastline of Quebec slip by. Black rocks seamed with
snow frowned down upon the river from the north, the
land had an aloof, forbidding beauty.

To us, coming from across the Atlantic, the Province of
Quebec looked to be in the grip of bleakest winter. A
smell of snow was sharp in the air when we hove to for
the pilot-launch from Father Point. Rivers swollen with
snow-water brawled down into the mainstream, rivers
with names reminiscent of Paris and of rural France: Port-
neuf, Milles Vaches, Cochon, Rivière du Loup; then we
were looking into the mouth of the Saguenay, spectacular
as a Norwegian fjord beneath a lemon-coloured evening
sky. Plenty of French saints, too, on the map: Saint Fidèle,
Saint Valuer, Saint Agapit and Saint Moise; we wondered
who they were and what had made them saints. And there
were names dating from long before the white settlers:

49

Yamachiche, Cacouna, Chicoutimi. At night many small unnamed fishing villages twinkled in the darkness from the shores of the river and by day their little houses looked like the villages of coloured wooden bricks Robin had left at home.

At the exact hour the purser had predicted, on a brilliant spring morning, our ship steamed past the Isle of Orleans and tied up below the City of Quebec. No trace here of the austerity which marked the country round Gaspé. The sun was shining and there was already the promise of warmth in the air. High above us, Quebec Citadel was bathed in light which had not yet reached the ancient balconied houses crowding together at the water's edge below the famous heights. Now we had scarcely time to find our friends and say goodbye. We knew we should land without loss of time, but could we get off that boat? We could not. Two friendly but opposing groups of men were lying in wait for Freddie, both equally determined. We came to know them gradually, they were all very kind —there were the blue-suits who were intent on getting Freddie's life-history, from birth till now, and pictures up on deck; and there were the others, present in a slightly more official capacity to help us with landing-regulations and make sure we left the boat as planned.

At first the blue-suits had it all their own way except that they disorganized each other. A picture was taken of Freddie leaning against one of the ship's life-belts—his life-history advanced a few years. But there was now a kind of race-game in progress between our cabin and the deck and through it wove those other passengers who were in the safe-keeping of the boat as far as Montreal. They had mostly seen *Colditz* yesterday, they had time on their hands this morning and wanted to know how much Freddie had enjoyed making it. Quebec City beckoned, somewhere out of sight waited that essential taxi, the sunlight had already travelled down as far as the foot of the crags, the Quebec pilot came aboard and the mail-bags left the ship, but less and less did it look as if we were about to disembark.

Back in the quiet of our cabin the life-history had just landed Freddie in Britain on a wet evening in February 1939. There was still a long way to go but skill and gentle tenacity seemed to have brought victory to the blue-suits when we were snatched from their hands and given to the Immigration Authority. For a brief moment both our children were with us in the same place and while that moment lasted we were eased down the gangway and on to Canadian soil, and somewhere on this continent, a fraction to the west, must be Stratford, Ontario. Behind lay that till now important ship, her name in letters one foot high, blazoned across her sternplates. She was a temporary home soon abandoned, and there right before us, drawn up before the Customs House, stood the largest taxi we had ever seen, shining black outside and sky-blue within. It would be untrue to say the engine was already running but it gave that impression. Such a car could have taken all of us, our baggage, and most of the possessions we had left at home and still there would have been room.

The sun warmed us now, a haze of green buds, not yet open, illuminated young trees with a kind of emerald mist. It was already spring here, the first of spring. The doors of the great car closed upon us and we were off, charging up-hill and worming our way through the narrow streets of Quebec. Our French-Canadian driver scolded us for-lornly because we did not stop, even for an hour, to see the beauties of the city he loved. Visitors to Quebec, he com-plained, never gave their time to it. To the left and right buildings flashed by we should have liked to see. We promised ourselves a visit on our return journey and then we had left the city and were out at once in open country, eating up the miles along a road reassuringly straight and wide.

From there onwards we chased the spring across French Canada as far as Montreal, gaining a couple of months on Gaspé. We pulled up once for a meal at a drive-in, where the trees were in first leaf. The boys caught sight of the river shining beyond its bordering trees and there was a cry for beavers. They could not wait for us to tell them the St Lawrence was too wide to give any scope to these peculiar animals, they ran as far as the river-bank over the fresh grass. They were halted not by their parents but by some birds which were new to them. Large flocks of grackles calling one another by the family name skirmished wildly among the bushes. Not French-Canadian blackbirds with strange light eyes and diamond-shaped tails, but birds which the boys had never seen before and never would see in Europe.

At Three Rivers every twig was in full leaf and on the outskirts of Montreal we lost the spring altogether. Here it was early summer and hot sun lit up the city blocks. Now was not the time to think of trees. We had come a long way from Quebec and, thanks to the skill of our driver, we had come quickly but it was already late when we were swallowed up in the cavern of a huge hotel. There the Stratford Festival took charge, up we went in an elevator and into a suite whose bathrooms were equipped with every watery gadget short of fire-hoses to delight the young. It was only a matter of seconds to discover the showers. We found we had thirty-seven minutes to put the children under the showers, feed them and persuade them into bed to rest between their long drive and the long night journey and to make ourselves fit to attend the party while they slept or were supposed to sleep.

It was a warm-hearted gathering downstairs, bilingual, and at first the talk centred round the special problems of French Canada, language, religion, culture, economics, etc. Our strangers' nerves were soothed by a gentle welcome, were we not new-comers to Montreal—new-comers of one or two days' standing perhaps? Too short a time to have got fully orientated. Weakly we answered, fifty minutes. The talk flowed on, easy and unhurried, touching on sailing round the coasts of Greece and in the Aegean, and the Théatre du Nouveau Monde, then Shylock the anti-Semitic Jew hit us a smack from the shadows. We had been alerted about him already months ago and foolishly dismissed the problem far too lightly, so he was still very much of a mystery to us who had as yet travelled something more than a hundred miles through Canada. No distance at all in the New World, hardly a step on this vast land mass, but far enough to see that here was ample space for all creeds and persuasions and unrivalled opportunity to raise a new generation rid for ever of barren prejudice, which arose in Europe as much from poverty and over-crowding as from religious differences. Envy of success, drive and enterprise which such conditions breed could have no application here. Yet here already was the breath of fanaticism as with an almost complete confusion of thought Shylock's critics voiced their fears and forebodings. What better way to recreate the whole tense situation all over again? Viewed objectively the idea was grotesque, in-appropriate as meddling with the black arts in a cornfield.

The party was over, we had wound up the children's circus, very active in the suite above, and boarded the CNR train for Toronto where Freddie was due at a Press conference at ten o'clock next morning. This train was larger than Robin and William had believed possible. A pity to be so sleepy in a train pulled by so gigantic an engine, too sleepy to investigate very far. When we told them that Stratford, Ontario, had the repair yards for these engines as well as a Shakespeare Festival, they gaped and subsided helpless in their bunks, asleep before they were tucked in. The train drew out of Montreal and rushed wailing through the dark. The villages of Ontario and the apple-blossom, too, had been slipping past the windows in the early sunlight for some time before their rumpled heads craned out over the edge of their bunks to announce cheer-fully that neither had slept a wink all night and was that noise really the train hooting?

Within an hour of setting foot in Toronto Freddie was deep in the Press conference. 'Shylock again,' he said in the elevator after it was over. *The Merchant of Venice* was the topic of the hour. Yet there was no sinister idea behind the production of this play, nobody had any such thought in mind. It stages very well and suited the Tent, the director and the performers equally. Moreover, an actor with any definite style cannot modify a character as yet unproduced and unperformed in the hope of soothing prejudice. To warn him off is like tampering with an illusionist. His work in progress is fragile and idle hands can easily damage it and go far towards robbing him of his unseen work, an unforgivable hardship to those who express their art by means of the life that is in them. The director and the director alone, in Freddie's opinion, had the right to shape the part to the production and fix it in rehearsal. No outside consideration carried any weight at all, quite the reverse—the outside issue more often than not disobeyed the laws of the theatre, as in this case. The picture of Shylock that controversialists were so eager to suppress had nothing to do with any actor, past, present or to come. It did not, in fact, exist. The part of the Jew as planned for Stratford's Festival would be ready on time, till then it was not on show and until then it was a secret thing, unborn; argument could only delay development and blur the finished outline.

Driving out of Toronto now, on the last lap of our journey, we had our first view of the fabulous Great Lakes which make such a promising pattern on the map. We drove towards our destination along the shore of Lake Ontario, then through the blossoming, sun-drenched countryside of the province. The hours slid by; we had been late enough in leaving Toronto and stopped for lunch at a wayside hotel set down in the middle of a garden and then the time schedule was in trouble again. Our guardians began to look the least bit anxious by the time their car reached Guelph, for the deadline today was earlier than yesterday in Montreal. The Festival Foundation's party in Stratford was timed for five o'clock. By mid-afternoon we were flogging the clock and it did not look as if we should make it; hurried calls passed between Kitchener and the Festival offices. Four o'clock, and Robin had subsided, rolled up like a hedgehog. Four-twenty, William was peacefully asleep too. Towns, farms with magnificent Holstein cattle, villages with German and Scottish names flashed by and the lilacs were in bloom in people's gardens. We fled through New Hamburg, but the name of Stratford, so long the main focus of our ideas, was nowhere to be seen, until it appeared quite suddenly on the road signs and all at once we were driving through the town itself, with the children waking up and asking if we had arrived and not believing it, across an iron bridge and up through an avenue of shade-trees. The car drew up before a compact red house which looked homelike straight away, set back from the road at the top of a grassy bank and guarded by ranks of tulips in full bloom. There beside the tulips stood two tall figures, Dr and Mrs Guthrie, so we knew we had arrived.

The time was ten minutes before five, but events which might have taken hours back home were telescoped, as in a dream—introductions, the Press, taking over the house from its owner, five minutes to see how everything worked, another moment, but only a moment, to admire the flowers filling every room, and the ice-box overloaded with all the delicious things any two small boys could wish to eat, though we were much touched by both kindnesses. William and Robin were due at a tea-party and we were overdue with the Festival Foundation. We were on our way and found ourselves in the president's car taking the boys to their destination and later arriving at a large wooden hall, newly built among willow trees, with as yet no glimpse of the Festival Tent. The hall was packed with Festival actors, Festival governors, Festival directors, all Stratford. We met old friends and found a multitude of new ones. But the day was not done yet. It had taken on a timeless quality, though strange transformations still went on. First Shylock had threatened to dwindle into a spiny little creature, then we had crossed Ontario with the urgency of migrating birds, and now the Festival party suddenly turned into a newsreel. More accurately, the leading players were caught on the wing and left the party early to appear in one, taken on the grass verge of Lake Victoria where the swans, who had become very camera-conscious, tried single-mindedly to get the best angles for themselves. In the background stood what we had come to find, the Festival Tent, immense in a green meadow. Its real size was much greater, even from a distance of two hundred yards, than any documentary could convey—only air-photography could capture the scale. Rigged from four towering steel masts, its wide sweep of terra-cotta pink awning and grey canvas walls gave it an air of having flown in from the desert. It could have been something designed for one of the Pharaohs by a more than usually enterprising tent-maker. There it stood and there it would be tomorrow—we had reached our destination.

The mysteries of our new home came at us next morning; we did not do much more than look at the flowers the evening we arrived. Hailing from an island where the open fire is much abused, but comes into its own from time to time because the coal for it is buried in our soil, we had no idea by what magic this building was heated. What was the giant humming in the basement and whence came the streams of air so warming to the feet? What was the cryptic dial above the electric-range and why was it slowly going round? 'That,' said Freddie, 'is a clock,' and so it was, a clock. Early on the first morning it looked like something quite different. It pretended to be making toast or timing pastry.

Robin burst upon us at breakfast time. He had finished first and gone outside. 'There's a rabbit in the garden! A real rabbit!' We followed him on tip-toe and found a young wild hare. It looked us straight in the eye and cantered off. We had hardly finished coffee before the child was back again, digging his nose into a fat, disgraceful bouquet, the front-garden tulips snapped off short, not more than three inches from the flower-head. He gave them to us. All the tulips? All but about five which did not take his fancy —but he had not finished telling us. 'I saw a squirrel upside down and its tail was much too big. There's a bird-box and there's a brown toad asleep in our flower-bed. It must be sun-bathing and its friend!' We poured a fresh cup of coffee and took it with us into the garden to examine the toads. Sure enough there they were, the two of them, blissfully toasting under the delphiniums.

5

FESTIVAL

For the new-comer in Canada two overwhelming impressions of the 1955 Season in Stratford were the Tent Theatre and the sudden, violent impact of an exceptionally hot summer, the hottest Ontario had known for years.

On a morning of brilliant sun, the first rehearsal of *The Merchant of Venice* in the Tent, over by midday, sent Freddie travelling in mind to a holiday in Greece—tantalizing—yet it was his way to conserve the best of the old as a framework for his new experiences. He might talk about the Greek theatre while he ate his lunch, but he was thinking over his first impressions of theatre in Canada. Meanwhile he told us the story of this long-past holiday when he crossed from Piraeus to Aegina in an overcrowded coastal steamer and voyaged on in a craft even less seaworthy as far as Epidaurus, his ultimate goal a theatre said to be the most beautiful in Greece. There he found it true that an actor whispering German poetry could be clearly heard from the most distant circle of the amphitheatre. Not since he had stood in this sun-baked marble ruin had he come upon a stage remotely similar.

Now, he said, Stratford had put a Greek theatre under the umbrella of a circus tent and peopled it, as could be seen within the first hour, with young, thriving and vital talent, any amount of it. For him the Tent presented problems of movement, projection, voice-production, as well as characterization, which were fresh and therefore much more absorbing than doing Shylock on a proscenium stage, and the comedians, he added, were a delight. Further, there was nothing that Canadian voices could not do with Shakespearean verse; the sense of poetry was there, the timbre right, and that was more than half the battle.

Waiting for rehearsal to begin, when the Tent was still dormant and almost empty, the impression it made was tremendous enough. It looked, if possible, even bigger empty than when it was filled to capacity. With hardly enough light to bring up the colours and what light there was focused on the pillared stage, it was impossible, until you became accustomed to it, to see where it began and ended. Was the great bellying skycloth blue or black, would it suddenly light up with stars—and the delicate bleached stage-structure, was it made out of wood or bones? And countless horse-shoes of pale, empty seats waited for the Festival to begin. This theatre looked as if it had been here for ever; that four years ago the ground it covered was part of a meadow and that some of the weeds in the grass outside were older than itself, was hardly credible.

The Tent had far more atmosphere and far less solemnity than a conventional theatre of comparable size. By simple association, this affair of canvas and ropes at first almost tempted one to expect that a troupe of Palominos, decked out in coral-red harness with plumes, would come trotting on, or that some imperturbable acrobat would appear to perform a death-defying feat, perfectly

Shylock Triumphant

Shylock Defeated

Diana Valk with William and Robin

timed. Canvas and ropes gave the place a life of its own. Doubtless it was as capricious in a high wind as a square-rigger and needed as careful handling by the tent-master. The fabric would not last for ever, this theatre would not be there for many seasons in its present dress, so goodbye to the Palominos and the acrobat. A chirping cricket, Iachimo's cricket without a doubt, auditioning tirelessly in the skycloth for a future production of *Cymbeline*, brought us back to Shakespeare and the rehearsal about to begin.

While the Festival plays were shaping in the Tent there was an explosion of life outside. All over Stratford and the country round, flowers bloomed overnight which took three days to open back in Europe, and this year the summer came so suddenly and so hot that most of the flowers were in bloom simultaneously, roses, flowering shrubs, hedges of peonies, poppies, beds of garden irises and the wild ones, ringing the lake like blue eyelashes. The whole riotous business could be seen condensed, on Saturday mornings, upon the flower-stalls of the Farmers' Market, a foil to baskets of eggs, shelled peas, water-melons, and home-baked bread. Robin and William, with the help of school and the public library, brought forth strings of new facts hazardous to parents, and a flood of questions was interlarded with the mysteries of Shylock's creation:

Q. 'Which bird can fly sideways as well as backwards?'
A. 'The Humming Bird, my teacher says so.'
Q. 'Where can I find a Box Turtle?' or quite simply: 'Why are there no Loons?'

Swans quickly took pride of place among the wild life available. There was the old cob who attacked and bit cars until he must have bruised his beak. He had a nest in a marsh below the rail-track and was invariably out of temper. Young innocence dreamed over her eggs upon an island site in the creek below the president's garden, and there was the witless pair who hatched a family of six, but when launching day came had no more idea of getting the cygnets into the water than they had of driving away two black crows who threatened their lives. The parent birds swam hither and thither complaining softly, the cygnets bunched together in a fluffy pile, and the crows perched on a nearby bridge ready, or almost ready, for a meal. If the crows were not in a hurry to eat, both parent swans were famished. At last hunger triumphed over fear and indirectly solved their problems. While the two crows drowsed, humped on the bridge-rail, the cob tired of the fuss and began fishing up water-weeds in long dripping strings. He ignored the squeaks of his family and ate them all himself. The cygnets eyed the feast, crowding so near the brim of their nest that the foremost overbalanced and fell, little black paddles waving like flakes of seaweed, a full twelve inches into the water. It reappeared right side up, dry, poised and confident, and swam away. Within seconds its brothers and sisters had pushed each other in and the crows flapped away baulked and disappointed.

A more complex establishment was that of the mallard duck. She hatched nine ducklings and swam daily on Lake Victoria leading her young family, with no less than three magnificent drakes in attendance, bringing up the rear.

On one of the first very hot days, when not a breath of air stirred the leaves, we sat cooling ourselves in the shade of the porch. *The Merchant* was going well, *Caesar* was in full rehearsal, and there was nothing Freddie need do until the evening of today. A certain serenity blessed this rehearsal phase. It was a time of withdrawal from the outside world, but within its own sphere working conditions could not have been bettered. The tension of three approaching opening nights was clearly to be felt but as an agreeable tension, slowly building up in the right direction. Futile crises which can so easily fret a theatre company did not exist and nothing of the gruelling stagnation that is like a fast walk on a revolving stage, in order to stay in the same place. Every rehearsal brought progress. The time of preparation was nearly over; given another week, a few finishing touches, the part of Shylock would set into its final form—a paternal man, confident of great wealth, with a caustic but by no means unjustified sense of humour. Tragedy overtook him in the latter half of the play, fruits of the injustice done to him, and he was broken finally by the treachery of the Gentiles. Goaded into his obstinate plea for the pound of flesh by worse men than himself, he put himself in the wrong with a plea for justice. Fundamentally he was too gentle a conception of the part to be a menace to the living anywhere, too sober to worry anyone.

We relaxed on the porch and talked about the part, wondering if the heat had come to stay, and waited for the mail to come. Idly we watched a family of squirrels emerge from the untidy lump of twigs that made up their nest in the middle of a hawthorn tree opposite our house.

They chased up and down the trunk and capered among the branches like skeins of black knitting-wool.

Idly we watched the postman visiting several other houses in the road. He came across to us and gave Freddie a stiff white envelope postmarked south of the Great Lakes and, as always, we admired his hat. When he had gone on up the hill, Freddie tore open his letter and here chance stepped in again, for this letter was full of solemn words to the performer of Shylock, speaking to him as to a wrecker let loose upon the New World. It was a very serious letter, seriously meant. We read it through several times feeling like malefactors; it was not the first of its kind but by far the most direct. What, in the face of such a lecture, was the actor to do? How even to answer a letter of this kind—with the story of an excitable stranger who burst into Freddie's dressing-room between shows on a matinée day of *The Merchant* years ago in London? 'I feel you ought to know,' the stranger cried, with more force than common sense, 'that I think the only thing wrong with Shylock was that he needed mothering!' Better not, though the tale was as true as it was far-fetched.

Had the true disciples of Freud, asked Freddie of his letter, intruded on the direction of *Oedipus Rex*, would the mothers of soldiers resent the implications of *A Soldier's Tale* throughout the Musical Festival? He stood up suddenly and the letter dropped over the sill of the porch and floated to the ground. A flash of white paper was enough to panic one young squirrel who had ventured as far as the roadside and sent the whole band scurrying up their tree to vanish into the nest. 'You see,' Freddie laughed, 'what this monster Shylock does to little squirrels?'

He went into the house without further comment, to fetch the book of *The Merchant*, and came out again at once with a sparkle of half-amused combat in his eyes. He recovered the letter, sat down and glanced through it again.

'From now on, I toughen Shylock,' he said, tapping the stiff writing-paper with his glasses. 'From now on I show them what Shylock is really like.' He checked over his part with the book, scene by scene, omitting only the first, working out where he felt new emphasis should come, darkening all its colours, tempering Shylock's pleasanter aspect and, where possible, driving more iron into his unyielding soul. A few extra points of light and shade, a punch here and there, the character stiffened, broadened, came out older, but that was by the way. It was all blocked out very quickly while five squirrels had their afternoon nap.

'And now perhaps when I have done with Shylock, the YMCA will protest. Christianity will be shown up in an unfair light, knocking him out. I toughen him,' he said, snapping the little red book shut. He certainly had and he went off well satisfied for his favourite walk round the lake. First to see what *Julius Caesar* was up to and then to try out his new version in the privacy of the Tent under the Director's eye.

Later that evening watching the Trial Scene, we saw a Shylock sketched who might have come striding down from some mercantile Mount Sinai ready to crack the tables of stone on the skulls of his tormentors. The reading of the part had gained very much in grandeur, its lines were bolder, the character far more drastic and also more distinct. Such are the fruits of argument with men who listen to their critics.

'They threw things! They threw things!' At the seventh and last dress rehearsal of *The Merchant* this horrified murmur, mingling disgust with disbelief, came from William, sitting staring down at the tempest on the stage, wringing his hands at the close of the Trial Scene, when Shylock was hounded from the acting area and driven down, apparently under the earth, by a mob of Gentiles as irresponsible as they were overwrought. Only a handful of people attended this rehearsal and the actors in their pool of light had to overcome the effect of nearly two thousand empty places, nevertheless the Trial Scene had a scorching quality not easily missed.

An inter-denominational service of dedication for the Third Stratford Festival was held the following Sunday afternoon, when also the season of parties began, and the evening after we were able to see the Tent Theatre in action for the first time, as its designers must have visualized it before ever the canvas was cut or its miles of ropes measured out, glowing under batteries of lights with every place filled for a great formal occasion. It is hard to recapture the rising tide of excitement on this first Opening Day of a new Festival Season. *Julius Caesar*, tonight's play, had never before been staged in a theatre of comparable size and shape, that much was reasonably certain. Shakespeare's Globe Theatre was also a theatre in the round, but it was a small building, in comparison with the Tent, very small indeed, open to the sky and fitted with balconies. The poetry had been written and the characters drawn three and a half centuries ago, yet the *Julius Caesar* we were about to see was a new play.

We watched the Festival audience streaming into the theatre until red-coated trumpeters lifted their trumpets to their lips, warning us to go inside ourselves. Summer dresses, gala turn-outs, it looked like a flower garden inside. Most of those in the audience had seen the first two Festivals. We were still the new-comers to their theatre. Its very size was comforting; here was an auditorium open to the world, large enough to seat more than a tenth of Stratford's own population at every performance.

Trumpets rang out, alarmingly a bomb exploded, signal that the show was on—then, in a moment, *Caesar* burst upon us. Roman artisans poured into the acting area, grumbling as was their way, and were driven off again. Imperial Rome followed them on to the stage, a changing pattern of light and colour. Political intrigue, Caesar's pride and uncertainty, soothsaying, conspiracy and murder hounded each other through the theatre. Tall figures in blue, crimson, grey-green leapt up and were overtopped in their turn by a parade of golden emblems.

Crowds massed and dispersed again, Cassius upbraided Brutus and Casca was greatly troubled by a thunderstorm. Conspirators knotted together in a tight, distrustful bunch. Calpurnia followed Portia in a hopeless attempt to stave off disaster from her beloved. Caesar fell and, lonely and distraught, Mark Anthony made us regret him. The pulse quickened and the action piled up into a pyramid with Anthony at the apex and the play exploded into war. Armies poured over and under the stage and chased up and down every gangway. Brutus and Cassius, lonely in their turn, quarrelled and died, and at the last desolate anti-climax of armed conflict unresolved the two surviving war-lords were left with all of Caesar's problems and none of his experience, blazing sombrely at one another across the empty stage.

Two thousand people streamed out into a Canadian midnight patterned with stars, people released and exhilar-ated. *Caesar*, known to many schoolchildren as a work of uninspiring samenesss patched with quotations, had quick-ened into a pagan battle-piece. The play spoke of Ancient Rome and belonged to us today. The heroes we had just seen have their counterparts living now, in Rome and in the Kremlin too.

'Hey!' called a dusty, carefree ten-year-old, a few weeks later, to his friend, blissfully rubbing a sunburnt nose against the fencing round the Tent. Groups of Romans stood round the stage-door, airing themselves, in full mag-nificence, between scenes to the great admiration of these children. 'Hey! Is *Julius Caesar* true?'

The second play of the Festival was the *Oedipus Rex* of Sophocles, now in its second season at Stratford. If *Caesar* brought out the dynamics of ancient history, *Oedipus* delved into still more ancient legend, dragging the audience in its wake, inwards and downwards into a suffocating domestic whirlpool. How else to describe this terrible spectacle of the wreckage of an ancient house? It has been said, and with how much truth, that King Oedipus is not a relaxing play. Staged at Stratford, Ontario, as a ritual, intoned by masked, robed and gloved figures, glowing or dark, stupendous or grotesque, it was still a family drama and, as such, tore at the emotions; something as malign could overtake any one of us. Shepherds, the chorus, messengers, all were part of or ancillary to the King's household. The seer, Tiresias, however alarming, was or had become a local man, dealing only in the problems of the court, and the masks worn by the players seemed to descend, however symbolically, upon us, the audience, and make us one with the complex ritual of the tragedy.

Two great days, one more to go and the new Festival was open. When we awoke next morning launching-time had come for *The Merchant*. The day began with cries of protest from our family. 'The brown toad has left, and his friend,' for indeed the creatures were gone and two little dents in the sunbaked earth where they had rested were empty. 'Perhaps they're hibernating?' We said it was too hot. 'Do you think they left because we are too noisy?' Happy thought! We decided to act on it and the two boys were sent off for a morning walk round Lake Victoria with a friend. The loss of the toads touched on a critical point. Quiet this one day had to be. If Freddie was to go on this evening and give the performance he wanted to give, then he must go into hibernation until theatre time.

Peace lapped the house for something over half an hour, then there were footfalls upon the porch below our room—William's footfalls but slow, quite unlike his usual scamper. At the stairhead he paused, pale, with sad eyes. He took his time to make the bald and simple announcement:

'Robin's fallen in the lake—on his head.'

'Is he hurt?'

'No.'

'Frightened?'

'No.'

'Where is he?'

'Downstairs.'

'Send him up to us.'

A smaller, stockier figure appeared, damp, serene and slightly streaked with mud. We put him under the shower. Our telephone rang and through the music of the shower we learnt that Freddie's correspondent from south of the Lakes was here in Stratford, in person, determined on a last-minute appeal to the actor before the show tonight. We turned off the shower and retrieved the child from the tub.

'Interviews, while my sons drown?' Freddie took a dispassionate view of problems and calamities alike today.

'I did not drown.' The reproach came with soft dignity partly muffled by a bath-towel. 'I was looking for a Box Turtle. I fell out of a tree!' So that was the story. We excused ourselves to the telephone and hung up, hoping to hear more. How were we to know that Lake Victoria is no more than sixteen inches deep? The telephone rang again, insistently. The child went and dressed himself in a wasp-coloured tee-shirt and the telephone rang and rang.

'No interviews before the show!' said the actor suddenly, an edge on his voice.

'Sorry. No interviews before the show—family reasons. Sorry. No.' We laid the telephone gingerly back on its cradle, put the lake out of bounds to small wet sons now

dry and went out in the air ourselves. We were both thinking the same thing—was today of all days turning out to
be one of those when life is lived on the lunatic fringe?

We came back a little furtively a while later. Any surprise might be preparing, perhaps a swarm of bees? All was
quiet through the long, warm summer afternoon. One son
flew a train of miniature gliders, citron yellow, carmine
and royal blue, mainly into the branches of the acacia tree,
the other fished them down again with a long flexible stick.
Once their fleet had gone aloft beyond recall they relaxed
on the grass after so much effort. The cry went up for their
favourite drink: 'Can I have grapefruit?'

'It's like a birthday,' said the elder, spreadeagled near
the border from which their toads had fled.

'Much too like,' agreed his brother, busy with a drinking straw. Freddie was still invisible and fast asleep when
two lovely young girls arrived on the porch willing and
ready to take the children canoeing on the lake, and the
children, with eyes like lamps, leapt at the treat. One con-
dition? No more duckings till after the show—accepted,
and the girls said, with soothing calm, they were both
trained for life-saving. Four young ones went off joyfully in
the direction of the water, and as they went church bells
rang out a carillon, an age-old Scottish lament:

'I'm wearin' awa', dear, like snowflakes in thaw, dear—
I'm wearin' awa'—etc.'

at all times an affecting tune. It played itself out, unhurried and silvery in the clear air, and went on to

something more cheerful. Freddie's voice, fresh and rested, started whistling upstairs. It's in the bag now—something like four hours' sleep—put on the coffee-pot.

'We have time now,' he called from above, 'to walk round the lake to the Tent.' Time? Yes, indeed, still time for a minor diversion—how would Freddie take the sight of Robin in an Indian canoe, probably standing up? We walked to the Tent round the lake; no glad cries of recognition echoed across the water, neither canoe nor any other craft was in sight. Up the meadow as far as the Tent. 'Come in the interval if I am not all right,' he said, breaking a long silence, and the stage-door slid to behind him.

After the Roman and the Greek plays the Venetian, tragi-comedy, morality play, or some kind of lyrical catherine wheel? *The Merchant* had something of all three perhaps, with the crying of owls and of cats and the sparkle of actual fireworks for good measure, a pageant of colour and light with a Portia straight from Botticelli. The play was in bloom this evening and once the action fairly started, there was no holding it. Scene followed scene almost as contrasting turns demanding quick response. Whether delicate or massive, it was a matter of quick succession and quick surprise. The Princes of Morocco and of Aragon counterbalanced one another more than ever they were Portia's suitors, Morocco coal-black, white-robed, a giant baying disappointed love, and Aragon, the pallid princeling disconsolate in his coal-black entourage, were brothers in affliction. The Gobbos had a little play to themselves. Antonio threw a dark shadow behind the lovers' glimmering white and Shylock, red-headed, red-bearded, soberly magnificent, was father to a daughter brilliant as a Persian miniature. The evening wore on. What had so often seemed a long play became a short one and the whole-hearted warmth of the reception at the end overwhelmed. Freddie had experienced many opening nights in many and most different places, but never one like this. From Lübeck to London his powers as an actor had been recognized, he had been acclaimed whenever he appeared, though with more reserve. There had been nothing ever before in his experience quite like this and the reaction of his first Canadian audience took him completely by surprise.

After midnight the tumult of the play was stilled, the stage bare, dressing-rooms empty. Shylock's red wig was on its block, his wonderful blue-green costume on its hanger, his knife lay among the jewels, and his actor went home in a state of slightly dazed elation.

When the last car had driven off, Lake Victoria mirrored only street-lights and the big white stars. One belated engine in the CNR yards clattered and wailed fretfully. Lights went down in the trees outside the Tent and in the theatre itself. The huge place was deserted for the night by all save the faithful tent-master and the most celebrated insect in Stratford, the cricket chirruping in the skycloth. Another Festival was in being.

6

OTHELLO

One long haul was at an end, Shylock had reached Canada, but the end of one story merged with logic and grace into another yet to come. With the opening of the Festival it was as if Freddie stepped out on to a tableland. Not till the close of the season should we have to leave the table-land for whatever lay beyond, meanwhile enjoy the prospect! But a Festival from its very nature must be strictly limited in time. It makes the utmost demands on all those concerned yet it does not last. The Stratford Festival of 1955 was to run for nine weeks, nine weeks to cross the plateau. An actor's future work has the great stimulus of being subject to chance, but it is also a matter of careful planning. So much attention must inevitably be focused upon opening nights that it can easily be forgotten how often an opening night is the first signal for departure. The actors must think of the next job, if they have not already done so.

In Freddie's case this had been under discussion almost from the day we reached Stratford. No sooner had we sailed for Canada than a request followed us out from Britain for him to play a season, chiefly Shakespeare, in Australia. So he had embarked on a phase of long-distance travel? Mileage was as nothing nowadays, so why not go round the world while he was about it? Yet the job in Australia would mean the best part of another year away from home, and travelling the whole family together would be difficult to compass. For ages six and eight Australia was definitely not the answer to Davy Crockett. The offer was debated back and forth across the Atlantic, then referred to Australia again, and by the first days of July nothing had been settled. In the meantime other ideas came up from the States, as various as they were vague; nothing crystallized apart from a strong wish to stay on in Canada for a time at least.

As soon as might be after the Festival began Robin and William went off to the Junior Camp at Kitchigami on Lake Huron. They left without a backward look and enjoyed camp life more than they had ever enjoyed anything in their lives. They came back to us twelve days later most reluctantly, bringing with them a hand-made felt mouse, the cast-off skin of a large beetle, a repertoire of stirring new songs, and about a hundred multi-coloured bottle-caps, the tally of their soft-drinks while away from home. These last were used as counters in a new absorbing pattern game played on the floor of the porch. While the boys were away our house was unnaturally quiet, so quiet that a cardinal bird which sang, invisible, in a neighbouring tree sidled down a branch one day in all its glory and whistled at us. Thousands of bees humming in the acacia tree at our back door left when the blossom fell. The oil-heater in the basement, so puzzling to us at first, had long been silent out of respect for the heat of summer. New plans hummed in the house instead.

Dates were reshuffled, then postponed in Australia, though the offer hung on, but how was one to reach Australia from Ontario? Across the Rockies to the Pacific and back to London by way of India and the Mediterranean— through the Panama Canal or direct from Britain via Suez? Too far in any event, Freddie decided, and went next door to work for Murray and Donald Davis at Toronto's Crest Theatre where there was a clear-cut plan of action; for Freddie was not destined to escape from Shakespeare's Venice so easily. No sooner was the Jew safely on his way than the Moor sprang upon us. *Othello* was the play chosen for the Crest, following Sidney Howard's comedy, *They Knew What They Wanted*. Both plays were old acquaintances, so now we knew what was the prospect on the further rim of the Festival plateau. If *They Knew What They Wanted* could be described as a green hill, *Othello* was one of Freddie's favourite mountains. Othello, like Shylock, had a lively case-history, but this was in no way relevant to the needs of Canadian theatre and had to be done away with, sloughed off like the skin of the Kitchigami beetle. *The Merchant* had been and still was the cause of argument, yet compared with staging *Othello*, *The Merchant* is a quiet, decorous affair.

Othello was unique in Frederick Valk's life as an actor because he played this one Shakespearean role more often in the original than in the German translation. Romantically beautiful and inspired though these translations were, they belonged to the nineteenth century and could never, so he felt, exactly reproduce the colours of the plays

Othello and Iago (Frederick Valk and Murray Davis). The Crest Theatre,
Toronto

Toni Patucci in *They Knew What They Wanted*. The Crest Theatre, Toronto

concerned. In addition, *Othello* was the only English text-book Freddie would ever consider using. He arrived in Britain with a fixed determination to master the language for the stage in the shortest possible time and, with a copy of this play in his hand, he set about it. For an actor to change his spoken language in mid-career is an operation as risky as cutting the tap-root of a plant, because a tap-root, once cut, can never grow again, but thanks to the Old Vic Othello and the Old Vic Shylock, more than to anything else, Freddie was able to strike new roots—surface-roots such as can support the largest forest trees and stout enough to anchor him to the English-speaking world. Most important of all *Othello* put his work as a classical actor safe in his own hands again. Altogether he appeared in four different productions of the play in Canada and Britain, as against one previous one, all-important because formative, at the German theatre in Prague.

The Old Vic's *Othello* in 1942 lasted, in all, for nearly eleven months. 'Ee, love, is it only once nightly?' asked a Burnley, Lancashire, millhand raised on variety, when the company were enduring all things at the dress rehearsal a bare few yards from where she voiced her motherly concern. This show overcame physical hazards, ranging from a black and gold set whose wartime paint could not stand up to wartime freight conditions to a brown man's make-up which came off only by degrees—'No extra soap except for chimney-sweeps', said the rationing bureau—but *Othello* rolled on and into town, where it was met by the critical salvoes of the London Press hailing 'the Moor at last'.

Shylock, Othello, Lear, Macbeth—Freddie valued them equally, with a possible preference for Macbeth, but when it came to casting, it was Shylock and Othello who came his way more often than the other two and Othello, a creature so unlike himself, was worked deep into his consciousness. Writing of acting, with special reference to Othello, soon after his first season with it on the London stage, Freddie summarizes his own approach to the profession.

The real process of acting has never been explained—it is still a wonderful mystery—we still don't know how it is done—how the acting machinery works. Can you teach the process of transfiguration? You cannot. Either you have got it or not.

A young actor takes the stage as the spokesman of Shakespeare, Schiller and Goethe, through them he takes wing, wafted up into clouds of feeling. He is a dedicated artist, a priest in the temple. It will cost him dear before he gets hold of himself. He has the need of expression but not the means. Only when an actor is ripe can he work with the poets in equal partnership. Meantime he must develop his inner self along with the technique of speech and the mastery of movement, till the hour comes when he can hope to render the poet's words together with his own poetry.

There is so much to learn, the actor must be the rider and the horse but he can neither see nor hear himself, what seems to him to be genuine feeling may not come over at all. Feeling must be analysed, disciplined and projected. How is an actor to do this? Only by the mastery of his stock in trade, movement, repose, projection and speech—above all he must be immediately adaptable to the auditorium of the theatre in which he works and theatres vary very much in size and infinitely in acoustics. But the fact that the actor's body, his receiving and transmitting apparatus, is the one and only material he has to work with, makes the problem more than complex and deeply fascinating. He must acquire a third eye to watch his own performance across the footlights.

The actor, going down, down to the source of all things, where he meets Sophocles, Goethe and Shakespeare, drinking the waters they have drunk, finds the same ecstasies these men have experienced. He finds the shadows of their children. He locks them into his body and gradually the shadows breathe with his lungs, live with the actor's heart! They are vampires eating him up from inside and the moment comes when he does not see any more with his own eyes but with the eyes of Othello or Macbeth. Then it happens that the hunchback grows into a giant of beauty or that the pallid awkward girl is more overpowering than Helena. But the crown of everything is work—work which is like bargaining with God for a glimpse into Heaven. . . .

Such a theory applied to such a play brings with it its own problems and that these problems did not get out of hand was due solely to the existence of the third eye controlling work in progress as well as in action. Indeed, without this high degree of objective control the theory is dangerous.

Often it is harder to work out of an old play than into a new one. To Freddie's theory of acting add the Central European approach to *Othello* and the going is tough indeed. Long before he was ever cast for the part, Freddie was steeped in the play. He saw it delivered with extreme, even mindless violence and when his turn came to play the Moor he was asked for an explosion of primitive rather than primary emotion, the portrait of a man run amok in face of a culture he was unable to share with any profit to himself.

In Central Europe, Shakespearean drama was nothing if not thorough. Every device known to stage presentation was available, great scholarship and, as time went on, the psychological approach. This last was always a hazard. It could lead to playing Othello in the dark on hands and knees. Where Othello was, as of right, the bad boy of Shakespearean melodrama and every licence given to un-reasoning emotions and outrageous behaviour, the two leading actors barely had the chance to act as colleagues, more especially when acute nervous tension was held to yield a better performance, an irresponsible practice under which many actors suffered.

Freddie himself escaped the worst excesses but he often told of one celebrated actor playing Othello whose Iago, in a frenzy of malice, snatched up a theatre fire-bucket from the wings and tipped it over Othello, lying prostrate in a fit. Drenched, Othello rose up in a fury, but his protests went unheard, the director liked the touch. Othello fumed and dripped while Iago spoke up for his own artistic zeal. He had the ready answer; his art had made him do it. Othello pleaded shock, pneumonia and loss of dignity all in vain, the bucket scene stayed in. Though the fire-bucket was returned to its rack, a leather bucket was quickly made for that production and the only concession to Othello's feelings was that the water in it should be warm.

And now here was Freddie sitting out on the porch in Stratford, Ontario, relearning *Othello* for all he was worth, with an occasional look into *They Knew What They Wanted* for light refreshment. During the weeks of the Festival, as far as work went, if Shylock was the stone, Othello's was the life beneath the stone, entirely separate but very much alive. *Othello* demanded long preparation and discussion and the opening date at the Crest in October looked at all times very near. As soon as a text of the play could reach us our house boomed with Othello's voice until the brick-work trembled, though happily not with the same effect as this had had upon a long-vanished neighbour back home, who overheard the merest reading of the words between us and was ever after unconvinced that this was not our own private affairs we were discussing.

Close on the heels of the drama came the Musical Festival, giving Stratford *A Soldier's Tale*, a concert, or the miraculous Bip almost every day for three wonderful weeks. It took place in the Casino, built like a giant Dutch barn near the lake shore, and the concerts, which included Bach's Brandenburg Concertos and the music of Mozart, Vivaldi and Schubert, amongst much else, had the additional charm of being easily heard from a grassy bank running parallel to the hall under the shade-trees, though, alas, overflow audiences in this picked spot were more than ever vulnerable to a feature of life in Stratford best known as 'fun with trains'. Railway engines came in, for all types of repairs, to the CNR yards less than a mile from the Tent. Their clamour could be heard by everyone in town and for the performer their distinctive voices were at times an unwelcome addition to his own. If birds could scheme for pride of place in a newsreel, these railway engines, first-comers to Stratford, had a living grudge. Once is a joke where twice can be too often, and they seemed bent on spreading anarchy throughout the Festival. Their wails and protests superimposed upon a Beethoven symphony gave astonishing tone variations. In open competition with a hard-working Shakespearean company, the effects were even more malign:

ANTONIO. In sooth, I know not why I am so sad. (Whoo-oo-o!)

Enter Caesar in his nightgown.
Nor heaven, nor earth, have been at peace tonight. (Chuff-chuff-chuff-chuff-chuff.)

CALPURNIA. Oh Caesar, these things are beyond all use? (Pshshh-h.)

LORENZO. Who calls? (Whoo? Whoo?)

As for Oedipus, least said soonest mended. Let Bassanio's Portia have the last word:

The crow doth sing as sweetly as the lark
When neither is attended.

Two new parts notwithstanding, there were plenty of
gaps in Freddie's work-plan, for swimming, expeditions,
for William's eighth birthday-party and many other
parties. The little boys, now brown as nuts, would cheer-
fully have spent whole days in the swimming pool. The
heat went on week after week, bleaching the grass and
discouraging the flower-gardens.

'We don't usually have weather like this,' said the people
of Stratford, which is exactly what we were always saying
back home, though more often from under an umbrella.
Towards the end of August cool evenings gradually began
and finally a nip in the air at night warned us that our
time was running short.

We asked the boys one morning where they would like
to go for a day trip. 'Kitchigami!' they cried in chorus,
adding, as an afterthought, that they hadn't seen any
Indians yet in Canada. So we headed for Lake Huron and
when we reached a little signpost marked 'To Kitchigami'
they nearly got out and pushed the car. All through the
deserted camp they quartered the ground like very old
men nursing their memories. Their father was shown every
detail, the 'very particular cabin, called Chippawa' where
they had slept, their bunks inside, the chapel and the dead
campfire, even the garbage-dump was included. They led
us down a sandy stairway to the cool, whispering edges of
the water, stuffed their pockets with carefully selected
pebbles and then marched us up the stairs again and

stood us in the lookout, the most beautiful place in the camp.

When they had seen everything and we had seen everything we set off to seek the Indians, bumping for some distance along an overgrown track through the Reservation at Ippewash while the children peered hopefully into the brushwood through the windows of the car. 'Not like the picture-books,' we warned though we need not have troubled. Not a soul was to be seen, not an animal nor even a bird. Motionless twigs on the bushes along the way carried little strips of cotton rag whose meaning could not be read by us. When we stopped our engine the silence was uncanny, an inhabited silence making us feel intruders without any right to be there. Eventually, to our relief, the car threatened to sink into a bog and we could reasonably turn back, for we ourselves preferred more open country and the Indians were clearly not at home today. No sooner were we out on the highway than there were the Indians, a family much like our own, with a truck. Honour was satisfied and we were free to drive for miles along the lake shore at Ippewash Beach. Silvery blue, vast and empty, Lake Huron murmured against the firm white sand, rather desolate, summer camps deserted already and shutters closed against the driving storms to come, but beautiful with quite a different beauty to that we enjoyed another day. One Sunday a dear friend drove us out to visit a more sophisticated spot on the lakeside—a summer retreat again but what a paradise. An entire little village of summer cottages was set apart on a green lawn nicked out of the forest, Lake Huron framed by trees in the foreground and, on the vivid green grass, one big white rabbit in the arms of a red-haired child.

Then, to be so near Niagara with a young family and not to see the Falls was impossible. One blazing day we drove out there too, passing through the peach farms of Ontario. In view of the lowering sky we spent far too long seeing the Canadian Falls and made our entry into the United States in the midst of a thunderstorm. When we were taken inside by the policemen on the bridge to have our papers checked, the question 'Where were you born?' struck the little boys as irresistibly comic. Even the frigid gaze of a particularly tall man wearing black glasses in the thunder-darkened office was hardly enough to quiet them though it struck terror into our hearts. A while later we stood watching ribbons of lightning play over the American Falls and a fitful wind swirl their spray across the canyon, blotting out the Niagara river.

'Is this America?' Robin again, eyeing the display with some misgiving. We told him, yes, he was now in the United States.

'But is it America?'

'Yes.'

'Then let's get back to Canada!' He went streaking away towards the car and we had only been out of Canada for an hour. Perhaps the lightning daunted him or thunder above the thundering water. Back at the Canadian bridge-head, we were waved to a standstill by the officer in charge there.

'Where were you born?' asked the Canadian voice.

In Stratford the cygnets grew big and gawky, young squirrels filled out to match their tails, our own children grew and, just as Canadian children were beginning to think of school again, so must they. One last never-to-be-forgotten visit to the CNR repair yards where they saw engines slung about bodily in mid-air, and in every stage of undress, and were invited up into the cab of one of Canada's largest, a transcontinental giant waiting for tests, and then it was time for the children to go back where they were born, for they had a date with a new school in Britain with far too long a waiting list to admit of breaking the date. Suddenly we were packing for Freddie to go to Toronto. The days of the last performances came and, too soon, the Festival was over, ending, as it had begun, by overwhelming us both. And if Freddie had not emigrated? Would any audience in his native country ever have taken him to its heart like this? Unquestionably no—nor would the colleagues have thought of giving him the apt and friendly nickname he enjoyed so much—'Shy'.

Directly the Tent was no longer in action the weather broke. Deluges of rain rattled deafeningly upon its canopy and ran in rivulets on to the baked earth surrounding it. Trees dripped, the sky was grey, and a wet Sunday followed the last evening of *The Merchant*. Outside shots for a Festival film were scheduled for that day down at the Tent, but outside work was impossible, and instead we took shelter within. Looking down into the amphitheatre from one of the entrances, we saw a dim grey pit, quite empty— a volcano, extinct now till the bright weather came round next year. In a few weeks there would be nothing to be seen but the bare rings of the amphitheatre. Tent and tent-master alike would be gone, the Tent struck, four tons of canvas folded and stored and the entire theatre packed away like a Chinese puzzle and battened down for the winter. Roaming round from gangway to gangway beneath the drumming rain, Freddie was sorry to leave it, as we all four were to say goodbye to Stratford. But hadn't our Stratford Adventure, more than anything that came earlier, given back what Hitler threw away? He thought for a long minute. 'Yes,' he said, 'and more—much more.'

7

CONVERSATION BY LETTER

Greatly condensed from letters between Frederick and Diana Valk (Toronto-London), September-November 1955.

Toronto

September 2–5

I woke up first at four o'clock and I thought: Now they are rolling down the plains of Canada with all the wooden houses and those porches. Then again I woke at 6.30 and I thought: They are still rolling but not much longer. Soon they will be leaving the train and go easily on to the boat and the sun will shine and the air be fresh and cool. . . .

Afternoon. You are now in the middle of the St Lawrence and the sun is shining and the wind smells salty and I hope you are not chasing our rowdies permanently, but lie in a deck chair and allow your dreams to float across the water. . . .

Report about my day? It was a good day, golden sun, golden green, all made up for a warm autumn. The squirrels very busy. On the street the pavement watered. Freshness. A car stopped near me. 'Want a ride? You are Mr Valk, aren't you?'

88

'I am going to the Crest Theatre.'

'You know the way?'

'Yes, thank you.'

'All right—goodbye.' I got a paper saying there may be a truce in Palestine. I had a lovely rehearsal, lunched and rehearsed again. The weather is radiantly beautiful. At the theatre I was told, they are looking for me all over London. Well I am at the Crest and it is good so. . . .

I wonder if this lovely full moon which hangs over Inglewood Drive shines over your waters.

The ship cuts through the sea. You are old sea-faring folk now, this is your second day aboard. Have you good weather? Glorious here. A squirrel just ran madly over the whole length of the red roof opposite, stopped at the highest part and began to munch an acorn—but only half, the other half went into the squirrel cold-store. . . .

How is it on the boat? Perhaps you have done the same as me, concocted a letter to be posted on your arrival in the Old Country. . . . It's a good life. At the theatre I feel like in my young days, say in Darmstadt, when I intended to storm the heavens. *Et bien*, I now make my second assault.

From Montreal towards Greenock

At sea. September 3–9

. . . Anticosti, Belle Isle, Labrador then follow the curve of the earth towards Greenock and it will get you home. Blissful honey-sweet weather, a day for leaning upon rails and watching the sun on the water. Now you begin to taste the salt again. . . . Out in the deep water in shining ice-cold weather—the first icebergs, a small one blue and glistening, shaped like a woman leaning over a baby, three more far to the north like two church towers and a rowing boat and the supreme one, a hundred yards long and a hundred feet high, shaped, the boys said, 'like a bobtailed lion' (Thurber lion), so white, silent and sinister it dazzled the eyes. . . . Robin roams the boat with the face of Genghis Khan saying, 'I'm bored of babies!' A large selection, they bring out the patriarch in William. He goes round tickling their toes and chatting with them. . . .

No more iceburgers, as Robin insists on calling them, but Sunday night, leaning out of the porthole, the sky was rippling with the Northern Lights, another thing I've wanted to see all my life. This one was white, crinkled and folded with occasional 'searchlights'. . . .

September 7. . . . Heavenly weather, at midday we saw the first gannet flying with her speckled chick. Four hours later the Irish coast lying like a dream on the water. Funny to think of us at Killarney a year ago, and of this tiny half-deserted country so stuffed with legend that the people have nearly all left and soon there will be no one but the angel on the Skelligs.*

September 8. We must have anchored off Greenock between 12.30 midnight and 4.30 a.m. Lying among a crowd

* According to legend, Lucifer fell into the Atlantic west of Ireland and the Archangel Michael, after chasing him this far, settled down to rest on the Skellig Rocks, sixty miles off the Kerry coast.

of ships with the Scottish hills beyond. The boys? Such are
their emotions that I shut the porthole. (Ship's rumour)
Two days ago we were fourteen hours ahead of schedule.
. . . The boat is loud with roaming hordes of excited
children—William in difficulties with a girl (aged about
five), to escape her very oncoming embraces he fled into a
deckchair—there she followed him. 'Shall I, by any chance,
know how to get you off me?' says William—'Oh, my
feelings!' Now Robin has appeared in a gold Huzzar's hat
he got at the party last night. 'Please go and do that to
someone else—not me,' says William, the Cavalier. At last
Venus left us and Adonis sighed with relief and went below
and put on a false nose immediately. . . . (Second rumour)
The Liverpool Harbour Board has refused to take the ship
tonight, so we shall be sitting on our record till tomorrow.
After lunch. . . . Packed and looking for the Little Island
(Isle of Man). Nothing but the everlasting length of the
Mull of Galloway.

4 p.m. Steaming past the Point of Ayr (Isle of Man)
where the Scots used to sail across and steal our dinners,
and the whole beautiful stretch of the Island was quite
close, clear right down to Calf Island. The North flat and
low, bogland, where the old Manx miser dug up his gold.
We could not see Peeltown, where the ancestral boats put
out when the herring boiled, but rising above it the two
mountains hiding our little green valley that they farmed
when they couldn't fish and southwards the cliffs of
Bradda guarding that fountain (for the Manxwomen), a
nice, cool fountain—so much better than Desdemona's

handkerchief.* The sun was shining on something gold up in the hills, either their famous gorse or a cornfield. Then a strange thing happened, the weather change which gave rise to all these tales of a floating island, etc., etc. The sun was still on the patch of gold above Peel, a rainstorm swept up over the Calf—a matter of seconds and the whole thing vanished—impossible anything tangible could be there. A voice at waist-height (Robin) at my side said, 'Is it magic?' So much for Ellan Vannin. Given a helicopter, we could have spent the afternoon there and dropped back on board for the night.

A wonderful evening—the rainstorm passed and the sky is full of stars, a warm scented breeze blows over the Mersey, not unmixed with oil. Lights from Cheshire twinkle, Southport ditto, ships twinkle also. Light-buoys wink and bell-buoys ring coming up the Mersey. Last time we were here it was black-out (1944) with grey gaunt ships full of poor boys filling the approach. Now there are thousands of lights and the Gladstone Dock is full of bright funnels.

10.10 p.m. . . . under the Liver Building and the clock shines too . . . opposite the landing-stage . . . tied up. The boys woke, they could see the quay from their bunks, I told them, England. 'Oh, nice, nice,' says William.

* According to legend, a wash in this holy well, which could neither be lost nor stolen, had the same effect on husbands as the handkerchief 'with magic in the web'.

'Well,' says Robin, rearing up a fluffy head. 'Is it raining?' Te traa gholl thie. (Time to go home—Manx.)

September 9. . . . Home . . . a long, slovenly journey. Boys in ecstasies over the beauties of the Euston Road. Robin crooning, 'I am so happy—happy.' Our place—warm, friendly, all prepared—a really rowdy welcome home bouquet, gladioli, half an oak tree, carnations, dahlias, etc. . . . boys digging up treasures: 'Look what I've found— we've still got . . .' a battered pair of cymbals—a red mouth-organ. Now they are asleep, for many hours, I hope.

A letter with details of Australia went to Stratford on September 3. *Antony and Cleo* (Shak:) and *Caesar and Cleo* (Shaw)—four to eight months and you choose your leading lady if you like. A big film starts here in November and might fit exactly . . . made here—location 'abroad'— name 'Zarak'?—no script yet.

Toronto

(In rehearsal for *They Knew What They Wanted* by Sidney Howard, at the Crest Theatre.)

. . . My life will be very static and without much variation. There is the street-car to the Crest and back, there will be long hours spent in repose, there will be little walks for little meals and little shoppings, but big rehearsals and that will be all. With other words it is all work. That is exactly what I wanted. . . . A blue sky and a faded moon, a week ago Lake Huron, Robin beetling about in Kitchigami. . . .

H

The work toughens. Marceau opens the Crest on Monday, Valk a week later. End spurt again. . . .

Now here is my answer to that definite offer from Australia. Basically I don't want to go. I want to stay and work in England, but it will take some courage to refuse. I wouldn't dream to go for eight months, nor by ship, another two months beautiful as it certainly would be. I am not too keen either on *Antony and Cleo* or *Caesar*, nor do I know of a good modern play except Ibsen or *They Knew What They Wanted*. I prefer good English films and to stay at home. What did you say? 'There's life too as well as the profession.'—How right you are! So you see, it looks like No to Australia, but I will think before I refuse. A good English offer will settle the issue at once. . . . Now you are home, how does it strike you and the Canadian boys? How does it strike them? Do they miss the wide open spaces and all that goes with it? Does Robin play under the table with his wooden train? See theatre and film.

London

What is the Old Vic doing? *Julius Caesar*. Very Japanese in the theatre, Gielgud's *Lear* and the Kabuki dancers. Lindtberg's film *The Village** the important thing to see. I took the boys to St James's Park. Those trees so carelessly arranged, fantastic ducks—on the Horse Guards Parade a Battle of Britain Display—two Spitfires and a black Heinkel all over swastikas, to the boys' delight. Holland Park and they instantly adopted Kitchigami tactics and

* Pestalozzi—the International Children's Village for refugee orphans in Switzerland.

built a house out of logs. . . . I have a story brewing but it's non-commercial. . . .

Toronto

I took yesterday a taste of Toronto and it was very pleasant—again one has the feeling that even this big town has been set into the middle of a forest. Big trees everywhere, concealing the houses—Lake Ontario shimmering in the distance. Skyscrapers and neon making a picture of strange beauty and grandeur, downtown concealed. Later a firework blew up over the Lake. It is a very wonderful view. Toronto has districts of real beauty and Parisian grandeur. . . . Back to my trees. It is wonderful to live completely concentrated on the work, which grows in quality.

September 13. (After the Opening of the Crest Season with Marcel Marceau.)

A most lovely opening at the Crest. Marceau exploded on Monday, the 12th—it was a grand First Night. He is a supreme artist. Happy rehearsals, tough work but how good . . . then off to the Women's Press Club. I shot off about Continental Theatre—well received. . . . I feel good after six hours' rehearsals. It's tough now—First Night Tuesday the 20th. But the colleagues are so precious, the working conditions and the famous Davis atmosphere so lovely and human . . . all has been said but the good things are inexhaustible.

The Island and Ireland certainly gave you a royal welcome. I got two long reports, 'Venus' and William, this beloved fellow Robin—I see it all. You must show me the Island one day.

It's so hot that the acorns are bursting in the streets with loud pops (squirrels disgusted). . . . Can you beat it, it's soon October and Toronto is like an oven—in spite of you being in a cool and moderate climate, I am enjoying a heat-wave. It is a shame, while groaning for the sun all the year, we come near to cursing her in Canada. It is a shame: the green is so beautiful and red and brown leaves are appearing more and more. For me there is nothing but work, only when *Othello* is launched there are free days.

. . . My acting develops on and on. Toni Patucci will be all right. I can now do things with ease, which were out of reach for me for a long time. I am a bearable actor now . . . serves me right. Why had I to be an actor? Technical dress rehearsal (not bad). Dress rehearsal (not too good). The whole Canadian venture will be a wonderful thing to remember.

London

September 20. (Before the Opening of *They Knew What They Wanted* at the Crest Theatre.)

. . . Pause before the First Night? All the work done and all you need to do is open the package and let fly what is inside. . . . Timing you all night, finally woke round 6.30 (1.30 a.m. to you) all tension gone. Now he's done it, 150 per cent. Breakfast, Robin beaming in with a letter and telegram, but I had the news already . . . How about Australia? I keep hoping it won't be—can't say why. I have got the tie-up for my story, the one I have been brewing for a year, that London Customs man out to suppress the liquor-trade from the Isle of Man (about 1720), historical incident and never written up as far as I know—surely one of our minor comic heroes. It is a joy to be writing again.

Toronto

(After the Opening of *They Knew What They Wanted*.)

Rehearsals for *Othello* start tomorrow and after that 'chaos is come again', but this is a holiday after the hectic First Night end spurt. As for the show, it was all right and partly very good. The first act was very nervous but very good. Acts two and three went beautifully. The box office is a riot, now for the final, with *Othello*. The trees are still green, some in glorious technicolour. Cool at last, thank God!

. . . Nothing much happens except work, but it is still a beautifully animated and young life. *Othello* moves on slowly and makes me incredibly happy with its glowing passion and tragic humanity. That marvel of a play which shines through all short-comings, fascinating to discover the measure of my development—artistically we can now reach out for what we wanted to get, an easy English has come with an economy of the means of expression and simplicity. It is getting tough with this man Shakespeare. . . . I am completely lost to *Othello*. I did it too early and that I wasn't smashed to smithereens was the merit of James Agate, who saw my possibilities and gave me time to develop. Now, I think I know it. Never before did I feel so stunned and blinded by a language which strikes me

like lightning and never before could I speak this language
—now I can. And this, together with my hard-won discipline and simplicity, may yield results I never had
before. Now let's hope we can one day transplant the
Canadian *Othello* to London.

It was a good trip and in spite of *Othello* my mind turns
to the way home, to be together again. I don't want to go
to Australia and probably I won't.

The entire company is happy with *Othello*. . . . I feel as
if I have met Shakespeare for the first time, which is like
living in the middle of an infinite orchestra. You have to
hold your head with both hands. . . . The squirrels are
chasing madly across the red roof opposite, sitting up, then
take a drink out of the drain-pipe and getting shocks from
the cold water. They peep into my room and rush off.
This whole Canadian job is a joy artistically. What a great
feast is this life.

. . . It looks like no Australia but a lovely cabin on the
boat on November 25, small changes of course are possible. Australia—it would be a strain, so at the moment I
mean no—like you there is something stirring in me that
does not want me to go.

. . . We rehearse in a church hall with a terrific din of
Canadian temperament. I wish you could see my Canadian Othello—I have got him now! No vitality lost but
discipline has come—which means many things I did
furiously and somehow irritatingly are now done quietly
(but full of sound and fury, none the less), great progress
of technique and my voice obeys marvellously. Apart from
the insight I have gained into the most marvellous poetic

language in the world. Yes—things do take their time and you can't anticipate.

. . . I shall not go to Australia. Just think, all my jobs in 1955 were outside England. It's not right to do the same in 1956. Moreover, I might go again to Canada.

. . . Yesterday the Comédie Française stunned me again with their décor and costumes and the century-old finesse of their actors—everything is technique, routine and elocution. Not my way of acting. Of course that heavenly *Le Bourgeois Gentilhomme* needs stylization.

On Thursday I have to speak at the Empire Club but I am free after that and go in the evening to see the Comédie Française (*Le Bourgeois Gentilhomme*) with Miss (Helen) O'Reilly.

She told me a charming story:

Her friend Lotta Dempsey, who wrote such nice things about me, introduced herself to a filing cabinet in which to keep the many papers which she needs for her writing. She had mislaid her notes about me and asked Miss O'Reilly: Where could those notes be? Under V? 'No.' Under F? 'No.' Wait a second, they are under D—Darling. Wonderful Canada!

I saw *I am a Camera* yesterday after fierce rehearsals. I got the usual shock seeing myself.

The speech (at the Empire Club) had a huge success. It was broadcast, papers printed it—this is what I said:

Every speaker worthy of his salt begins his speech saying that he is honoured to be where he is. If I say that, I really mean it. I don't want to say that any speaker who says this

99

is insincere, this is certainly not the case. It may be a phrase but it is certainly not politeness with me. I am greatly honoured to have been invited by Dr Goldring to appear here at your luncheon, and face the Canadian men and women of whom I have become increasingly fond.

I came over here in May with my wife and my two little boys who have since returned to London and we have really had one of the most happy times of our lives. Canada and the United States were nothing but an idea to me up to now. Everybody is told so much of the way of living, the mental ideas of a foreign country, that he is curious to find out how these ways really go. But from the first step on the boat, I may say, I was surrounded by friendliness, goodness, and had a real welcome, and while I was at Stratford, people did all they could to make me feel at home. Here in Toronto I have suffered from my bosses, of course, but apart from that I am frightfully happy to play at the Crest.

Now it is said that those who talk so much on the stage shouldn't talk too much in private. No Artist should talk at all, he should let his work speak for him. Above all, I think, that talking, making speeches, especially in an illustrious assembly like this, is an art in itself. It was considered so by Greeks and Romans who had wonderful symposiums on one theme, profound philosophic matter, Art, Architecture, Poetry and Music. This way of speaking, of making speeches to friends, people or guests, has not been lost altogether, it is highly cherished in English-speaking countries—less on the Continent. To be called upon to speak at the Empire Club, succeeding many very illustrious men who had the ability and the knowledge to talk about special things, was quite a task for me. I have never made speeches before. I took the jump and had a dress rehearsal with a speech at the Women's Press Club of Canada, where I was frightened to death, but they were very gracious to me and said it was all right, I shouldn't be frightened. So I take it a little bit easier today and I hope you won't stone me.

What shall I talk about? Everybody should only talk about things which he understands, and I think one of the very few things that I know a little about is the theatre, and acting, the art of acting—if it can be called an art—and the organization of the theatre. . . . You may not always agree with my opinion, but allow me to speak in the way I think and feel about things. Talking about the art of acting: here I always feel, this is a subject so complex and in a way so profound that it is not yet entirely understood, even by actors. If somebody says acting is a second-hand art, he is right in a way. Not completely right. We actors are speaking the words written for us by somebody else and we live on borrowed emotion which we assimilate within ourselves and then project. But what somebody else did write has to be brought to life. Putting on a false nose and a synthetic face will not convince people that you are Richard III, or adding stuffing and sticking many hairs on to your chin won't make you Henry VIII. All that is impersonation or performing, which is not acting. Acting is something mysterious and indeed something very profound. It just happens that an actor—if he is an actor—though he be a short man, can possibly play, say, Don Quixote, who was supposed to be very tall. The actor really grows, he changes from inside and somebody who has to play a fat man, though very thin himself, gives the illusion of fatness. It is a mysterious act of transformation. Acting, as I see it, is amalgamation with the idea of the part, mixing it with ingredients of the actor's own body and soul, growing into the part by a sort of trance and trying to project that. It is not pretending to be something, not performing but just *being* the part. One has to *be* Richard III, Henry VIII or whoever it is. And finally begins the technical process of projecting the part into the audience. Only a few words about that. You have a theatre holding, say, a thousand people and you must project your Richard or your Henry into that room. If you do a radio-show, standing before a microphone, you project over a distance of about two yards, in the theatre the projection is over about forty to fifty yards. It is obvious that all this is a matter of speaking technique, breathing and concentration. An actor must be able to control firmly his technique of projection. He must have two, rather three, eyes. The inner eyes and the outer eye. Two eyes to see the idea, to imbue, to amalgamate the idea of the part; and a third eye which is before him, having the task to control himself. This third eye is the actor's conductor, controlling his projection with everything that belongs to it: Voice, facial and bodily expression and the underlying emotions. The third eye continuously watching his own actor, is the all-important control-point.

You see, it is quite a complex thing and I maintain that

the Art of Acting has not yet been analysed. Lots of things have been said, but mostly about performing, or some form of presentation, but there doesn't exist any scientific analysis of the Art of Acting and if I use the word Art I mean it with all its implications: Form and Life! Every acting part contains not only emotion, violence or sweet music of the heart—a form belongs to it as well. Nothing vague must be sent into the audience, only complete and clearly defined parts.

That is all I can say about acting at this moment, though I could go on for weeks. But I must say a few words about the theatre.

You all know how it began. It started with the Greeks and its glory, power and poetry has never been surpassed. You may have heard Sophocles talking to you in Stratford, Ontario.

The Greek theatre was of course a religious celebration, profound and mysterious, clad in stories sometimes as melodramatic as a thriller. But these legends, these stories went to the roots of things, and Art is at the roots of things. You may choose other names if you like, you can call it religion, love or god, but if any writer is going down to the roots, holding in his hands the flaming torch, fetched from that source, he must have lived in the vicinity of Shakespeare. An actor who is blessed with the possibility to play Shakespeare is a person very much to be envied. There were the Greeks and the medieval church-mystery plays on the market places, burlesques originated in their rather crude and wild shows, and then the feudal lords took an interest in shows, had their companies assembled under their protection, sent them out or had them play in their halls for the pleasure of their guests.

Here we have the bargaining of the subsidized theatre. The great Elizabethan Lords patronized mummers and playwrights. Later the Continental Princes did build their huge and beautiful court theatres, paid for the entertainment of their guests, provided funds, so that the actors could rig up their shows, have their costumes and a little pittance for food. They were not regarded very highly, these actors and musicians. They were considered to be something like stable boys or lackeys and were treated with contempt.

There is a fantastic story of the eighteenth century. A Grand-Duke of the German Principality of Hesse-Cassel had in his Court Orchestra a drummer with a salary twice as high as any of his colleagues. The drummer had no hair and the Duke, from his box directly above the orchestra pit, spat at regular intervals on the drummer's head during musical performances. And for that fact the drummer drew a double salary. Musicians and actors were kept like dogs.

Mozart has no grave. He was buried in a pauper's grave and nobody knows the spot. Many artists of world importance starved to death in Germany and all over the world. Shakespeare, though, had enough sense, besides having the genius which he used to write his plays, to make a comfortable living.

Has this general plight altered very much? It apparently has altered, but not decisively. Let me first go on talking about the princes; you have at the moment in this town the Comédie Française, which is nearly three hundred years old and was from the beginning a subsidized theatre. Louis XIV made it possible for his privileged writer Molière who, by the way, had not a very rosy life either, to play his plays in some royal hall which was put at his disposal, and from that the Comédie Française developed. Royal money paid the company, it was royal money that fitted out the plays, and very little royal money paid the immortal Molière. And as Louis XIV gave the example to all Europe, Germany, Austria and Russia developed the fashionable idea, that the great Duke, the Prince, the Emperor, the King must have his court theatre, magnificently endowed, beautifully built, to entertain his guests —the populace was excluded.

Though entirely on feudal lines, this was a most important and wonderful thing to happen. It was the same spirit that provided the facilities for Michelangelo, Leonardo and a thousand others to create. It was the great age of the patron which was followed by the Kings and Princes of the eighteenth and nineteenth centuries, when every little princeling and every little king and emperor had his opera—or playhouse. In 1918 many crowns rolled down into the sea and the court theatres were taken over by the State, which considered it as a sacred obligation to keep these theatres going—for the benefit of the people. The State, recognizing the educational and cultural importance of the theatre, placed it in the same rank as church and university and supported it. Further, it was obvious that the theatre was above all a place of entertainment. Ideas are best digested if they are presented in a palatable way. You can say something profound in various ways: with a beastly seriousness, or in a battering way, you can say it jokingly, or in a frivolous way, but if the idea comes through clearly, every form is justified. Your man in the street, hearing in the theatre things of life and death, of God and the devil, of the above and beneath is not always able to take all that wrapped up in too rarefied a form. That is the value of entertainment, among other things—the easy presentation of things which are not easy at all. Every sort of entertainment, if it is in bearable taste, has the right to be put on to the stage. People are frightened away from the theatre if it is grim and serious, tragic, thunderous and pompous all the time. The Greeks understood that very well and threw their farces into the arena for the sake of relief. The theatre has to be not only university and church but a place as well to find entertaining joy, relief and relaxation.

We have now, all over the European Continent, theatres which are subsidized by the State, by civic communities or other corporations. It is logical and a sane policy that the theatre should get support through public means. And it needs only a fraction of the amount which is spent on things like transport, health services, museums, universities and other public institutions. The Vienna State Opera, destroyed during the war, has been rebuilt and princely endowed by State means—not a bad investment at all. You see, it is by no means a Bolshevistic idea to let the State take over in certain cases. If the theatre wants to sell something which is of a good quality, it must have its price. But there is a limit to what the public can pay, therefore support must come from outside, at least until the theatre can stand on its own legs. Max Reinhardt in Berlin was in a position to keep his theatres without any State subsidies, but he had to fight and to borrow money. And so had Stanislawsky with his Moscow Arts Theatre. There had to be funds to keep the theatre going until the public had taken it to its heart. No museum could exist on its own if you asked, say, $1 or $2 from the people for the privilege of seeing the skeleton of a dinosaur. The public wouldn't come and without State support the museum would have to be closed. It's exactly the same thing with the theatre and it is to be hoped that no dinosaur skeleton will ever appear in a Canadian theatre.

But the Canadian theatre has to live and no State aid is at the moment apparent. So the support has to come from the paying public. Canada is a young and wonderful country. Canada can look forward to an exciting future. It has immense riches, unheard-of possibilities. Because of its youth it has had no time yet to build up a theatrical tradition—it had to look first to the development of its industries and its material basis. The Canadian theatre will come quite logically, you can't live on lumbering and industry alone, the muses have to come in. I am happy to have played at Stratford—it was a revelation and I am happy to have met Murray and Donald Davis, the directors of the Crest Theatre here in Toronto. Here are two young men to do it, to build up a theatre, a Canadian theatre. They have established the Crest Theatre. They are presenting the finest plays. They pay the greatest compliment to their Canadian countrymen in giving them not the cheapest but the best, and I think that we have here the beginning of the Canadian theatre. They, more than anyone else, need all the support they can get.

I am profoundly convinced that Canada's theatre has a future, because I see how the people take to it, with their minds, thank God, uncorroded by over-sophistication, with their spirit of mentally alert children. Look at the faces of the people and you are bound to come to the conclusion that the Canadian theatre is a necessity. Time marches on—unfortunately—so may I end with this wish: As you are all prepared and desirous of the blessings of the theatre (I can't think of any State of any cultural stature without the theatre), may you get it, and may you get it from Toronto, and I think you will get it from Murray and Donald Davis.*

. . . About *Othello*—big rehearsal today in costume—it will look well, beautiful costumes, a glowing gold overcoat with a black collar—a white nightie with a grey-white over-thing.

Othello develops into a marvel. I herewith say the proud word: I am able to play him now.

London

(Before the Opening of *Othello* at the Crest Theatre, October 25.)

. . . A wonderful photo arrived of you in an Empire

* Reprint of a talk entitled 'Theatre in Europe and the Americas' given by Frederick Valk to the Empire Club of Canada on October 20, 1955.

nightie and what a most beautiful Desdemona. By the time you get this *Othello* will have, in Robin's words, zoomed. Nothing more about *Zarak* yet. Glad of the Australia decision. Somehow I did not like the idea—too far—too lonely—too strenuous.

London

October 26, 9.30 a.m. (4.30 to you). Now the bolt is shot, the tears have been shed and all is well. I stayed up working till I knew you were in your dressing-room and that the Crest had you safe—then heartlessly and peacefully slept till morning; before I woke, sometime after you got to bed, I was told in my dream: 'It has been a great effort and it has cost a lot, but it has been very much worth it.'

Toronto

October 26. Here is the incredible harvest (Press notices, etc.). I am half-stunned but very happy and healthy. 'Explosive—Atomic—Volcanic'—frightening. The great thing of it is, that it was done legitimately, not by ranting and roaring, but by a deep amalgamation with a power called Shakespeare—done by an actor who now can speak English and has the mastery of his means of expression, especially the voice!

. . . So much talk about *Othello* and so little about your work. I am so happy you are writing. There are lots of possibilities in the stuff, which your hand will exploit. I can't wait to read it. . . . I sail in three and a half weeks' time, hope to get that *Zarak* and glad if I have not to go to Morocco.

London

... now the Post Office thinks I have too many letters
and is putting them on to boats instead of tidily into aero-
planes—fabulous reports, but if ever anyone needs a T-
bone steak it is after watching your Othello, be merciful.

About *Zarak*. It is a deal and it has been sticky, a six-
day guarantee from December 14 plus one week on location in Morocco from December 1. You will have to fly
home, say, November 25?

Toronto

(After the Opening of *Othello*.)

Yesterday came that eagerly awaited letter of yours.
Here are your questions answered:

Murray*—quite excellent in devilry—a very good performance. Barbara† released a wonderful dramatic temperament. I could play Macbeth to her Lady. The
audience is hushed and overflows the theatre . . . all is
good and glorious and home will be heaven. Stratforders
are coming, though the show ends so late there is little
chance to see them afterwards. . . . *Zarak* has clicked.
Hurrah! Not many more letters will go. I come in person.
Othello's occupation's gone. Haji Khan's occupation begins (Haji Khan—Zarak's film father). A new morning
with you and the boys rises from the Atlantic. I must find
a suitable plane in case I have to fly. No problem, as they
say in Toronto. How happy I am. I wish the day had sixty
hours!

* Murray Davis.
† Barbara Chilcott.

PART 3

AFRICA

8

LETTER FROM MOROCCO

DECEMBER 1955

At home, in Britain, our telephone rang.

'Mr Valk?' The caller was our old friend from the tax-gatherer's office. 'Mr Valk, please.'

'He's in Africa.'

'Africa? You said he was in Canada!'

'That was last week. He was back in England four days but now he's in Africa.'

'What took him there?'

'Location work for a picture.' The voice at the far end of the wire warmed perceptibly.

'Another picture? What's this one called?'

'*Zarak.*'

'Funny name—where'd he go in Africa?'

'Xanen.'

'You did say Africa?'

'Xanen—in the Atlas Mountains.'

'Shannon's in Eire.'

'Not Eire—Morocco'—the land of the Moors, don't say it—grouse-moors—worse confusion, try spelling, 'X-a-an —back next week.' Too late; with a snort of incredulity the line went dead, our caller had hung up in disgust. And indeed it was more like three weeks before Freddie was quit of his new picture. But credible or not, eleven days after the last performance of *Othello* at the Crest Theatre in Toronto, Freddie was rubbing shoulders with the Moors of North Africa. Arriving on location for *Zarak*, after a hurried flight via Madrid and Tangier to Tetuan, the first thing that met his eyes was a detachment of Moorish Lancers; spectacular ruffians, beautifully mounted, with glittering lances eight feet long. They had been engaged not as film extras but to keep order among the hundreds of Arab poor needed for crowd scenes.

The postman came soon after the tax-man gave up and a handful of letters postmarked Spanish Morocco flopped on to the doormat:

. . . Where to begin? Tetuan? The film? They left the location too late, it is rainy, foggy, no sun. The sky is overcast—they can't shoot. I think I shall sit here for days, doing nothing. I don't mind and take it as a holiday. The country is rolling hills, it is green, the air is lukewarm.

The town is oriental, with some semi-modern streets. I went to the Arab shopping streets enclosed by the ancient walls (modern Tetuan is outside these walls). Picturesque —indeed picturesque, but oh, so pitiful. As a boy I would have thought to be in the one-thousand-and-one nights, as a man I see the human tragedy as well.

I thought only sick cats and vermin could live in these streets, but the Arabs really live here, diseased and unbelievably dirty. They crowd together in their little stinking shops, which are really holes in the wall, they sell dirty food or pottery or leatherware or what have you. They are slumped down in sinister cafés, smoking from long holders—and they don't look nice. Under the layers of decades of dirt, under deformities and all kinds of sores and behind blind faces, sadness, bitterness and anger is housed. If you lodge a people worse than cattle, how can you expect them to be merry as spring lambs? When an Arab brushes my shoulder in the eternal throng I get a shock and would like to scream for a disinfectant. The women are veiled, dirty and unbelievably unattractive. Soldiers and police are everywhere, wearing turbans or the fez—it is Franco's country and that of his beloved Moors. . . . They have the faces of murderers and seeing a sentry with his bayonet planted on his rifle is no joke. I still should see the Kasba (which means fort). It is in the Old Town, though after the Arab streets it won't have surprises. I should see the Jewish quarter which, by report, is lived in by people who have nothing to do with international Jews. Maybe the sun would make things look better in this little section of the Orient. I seem to have seen it all— I don't want to see more. Canada appears, looking back, like an antiseptic laboratory and the people like archangels.

But these are only the first impressions, they may improve. . . .

. . . I am in Xanen high up in the mountains, a lovely mountain resort—a luxury hotel as headquarters. The country is like the Lake District in England and green. It is rainy and shooting is doubtful, the hills are wrapped in fog.

Yesterday I went again through the depressing Arab Bazaar in Tetuan, no one will ever convince me of the charms of the Orient. Soldiers everywhere in this country and the terrific and abominable Moors with most picturesque and incredible uniforms (the regular army look like beggars). The depressive air of Fascism weighs heavy on one's chest. This country has no surprises for me, neither its beauty nor its dirt nor its poverty. We have read so much, seen so much, thought so much that with imagination we can see it all, I believe even Russia or China. Canada had surprises for me and its people, with their innocence and new outlook. So there is hope that some places in the world may still surprise and that the great things of Art and Nature will never be exhausted of their beauty.

The sun comes out a bit now and it is very beautiful. There is a little Arabian market opposite the hotel, fresh and quite different from the streets of Tetuan. . . .

We went still higher up, into the valley surrounded by craggy mountains and there was *my* film-village of huts and tents. There was a caravan consisting of camels and mules and music-playing Arabs, there were some wonderful horses of the Moorish cavalry which kept the crowd in order and there were hundreds of beggarly Arabs doing crowd work, there was the paraphernalia of the great film day with its real workers, and all the hangers-on, there was everything from a thousand-and-one-nights except the sun and so I have to go out again tomorrow morning. I have a little scene to play and I think that's all for me and Africa.

. . . This is the third day in my valley high up in the mountains and still not much happened. There was a long shot of me coming out of my house and meeting the Major (Michael Wilding) on his horse and then the rare sun was used up for camel caravans and infantry.

. . . Today is a bit better. It was raining on the way up to Xanen, six thousand feet up to my superior house in a meadow. If it rains I sit in a car, eat a sandwich, smoke a cigarette and wait, give autographs to Arabs and write to my wife. Little Arab boys peep now and then through the windows of the car. Now the sun peeps out, there may be some shooting. I have still to speak three lines to the Major. If they will then send me home immediately—it can't be long after. I have not the spirit of enterprise to stop in Spain which is so near and see that country on the way back. I want to be home at last and Spain is severe, even sinister with its Fascism. . . .

. . . No more sun—in my car—in my valley, we worked with the aid of giant reflectors, the Major beautiful on his white horse and I threatening him mildly. But it is not finished yet, I have to come out here again tomorrow through the dark mountains which are so beautiful. . . .

POSTSCRIPT FOR GERMANY

A translation of a talk by Frederick Valk broadcast by
the German Section of the BBC in May 1956.

I look back upon my Canadian journey with warmth
and joy. Humanly and artistically the experience was
equally precious.

Stratford, Ontario, is a lovely little town, at most a
hundred years old and still bearing the imprint of its
pioneer days. The main street has pleasant shops, a few
restaurants and soda-fountains. In the residential part of
the town the houses are as if set down in the original
woods. Small, pretty houses, huge trees tower above them
far older than they are themselves. There is a lake flanked
by many willow trees and on the shores of the lake, in a
green meadow, stands the Festival Theatre. A gigantic
concrete amphitheatre built to house nearly two thousand
people is enclosed by a monumental circus-tent slung from
four slender masts.

There, from the morning after my arrival in Stratford,
I rehearsed *The Merchant of Venice*. This is theatre in the
round, a great circular arena-stage backed by a relatively
small pillared structure. Dr Guthrie directs: flamboyant,
expansive, colourful. He peoples the arena with a master-
hand, his able supporter Tanya Moiseiwitsch, with her
firework costumes. Should there be more than two actors
on the stage together, the producer keeps them on the

move, giving life to the action of the play together with the possible danger of unrest. The actor on an arena stage like this one must inevitably move about more than he does within the proscenium arch, in order to be visible to all the spectators in so large an amphitheatre.

This kind of theatre lends itself to plays with large and colourful crowd scenes rather than to Shakespeare's domestic dramas, plays with many solo scenes, as in *Othello* and *Hamlet*, are at a disadvantage.

For myself, who had hitherto worked almost exclusively on the proscenium stage, the new kind of interpretation required of me by this theatre in the round came as a liberation. Monologues which had hitherto been delivered standing still, or at best broken up by only a step or two in either direction, developed into lengthy walks. This gave new life to the character and it felt like acting in the fresh air, in the open. This feeling of release heightened the tempo; whether clarity and intensity were always correspondingly enhanced is another matter. No fault was to be found with the acoustics but perfect speech technique was required of the actor. Whichever way he looked he was obliged to stand with his back to one section of the audience. The angle from which the public saw the show gave rise to another problem. It was magnificent viewed from the centre, directly opposite the pillared stage. From there one could enjoy the crowd scenes massing, the interplay of colour and movement or the mathematical accuracy of the different actors' positions on the stage which were sometimes overpowering in effect. But if you sat to one side the logic of the production plan tended to be obscured by masking and overlapping. The accents could at times be minimized instead of stressed. That an actor often found himself only a step or two from a member of the audience also endangered the illusion.

I fell in love with this stage and quickly adapted myself to its demands. The immense arena and the vast scale of the auditorium opened up new vistas of uninhibited performance. No more reticent diminuendo. No more underplaying. One felt as if on a raft in the middle of a lake with the right to plunge in and swim to the utmost limit of one's powers and energy.

It was in no degree necessary to shout, the acoustics were, as I said, good enough. Given the movement possible on this stage the whole rendering of a part, acted hitherto on the proscenium stage, had to be fashioned anew. Every detail had to be reproduced on a simpler, stronger plane. In such a playhouse only things direct and fundamental can come over. Emotion and passion carried, sensibility and sentimentality alike were swamped.

It was tremendously hot in the summer of 1955, more especially inside the Tent, in defiance of the air-conditioning plant. The men in the audience sat with shirts open at the neck, women fanned themselves with their programmes and the actors tried to freshen up under the showers or near the ventilators, but the warm ungrudging response of the public was a priceless reward.

In September I left the Festival Tent at Stratford for the Crest Theatre in Toronto, to play in *They Knew What They Wanted* and later in *Othello*. The Crest is a proscenium theatre with eight hundred seats and there I had to abandon my newly developed arena-style and scale myself down to fit a smaller range. Once again I was able to develop a monologue in repose.

The Arena in Stratford and the Crest Theatre in Toronto mark the beginning of Canadian Theatre. Canada —almost a continent—is the land of the future. Incredibly rich in natural resources, it has as yet had insufficient time to fashion its own abiding tradition of the Arts. The material foundation of the country has been laid—industry, agriculture, primaeval forests, minerals, hydro-electric power. The country advances with impressive speed though the population is only fifteen million. Now the cultural genius has awakened! The first challenge came from Stratford, which stirred up the entire country with its enthralling productions, and now the great city of Toronto has received its first professional theatre from the hands of one family, who have carried the theatre venture in Canada another step forward. They have a thousand problems to handle but their courage and initiative have given Canada a cultural theatre and Canadian acting is full of vitality and enterprise and individually brilliant. Further, a great international Festival of the Arts, something after the manner of the Edinburgh Festival, is planned for the near future.

Canada has left the first steps of youth far behind and is advancing with giant strides towards its own national theatre culture.

EPILOGUE

An Obituary of Frederick Valk which appeared in the
Peterborough Examiner, Ontario, on July 25, 1956

Thousands of Canadians have read with regret of the
sudden death of Frederick Valk, the Czechoslovakian
actor who was the star of the Stratford Festival in 1955,
playing the part of Shylock in *The Merchant of Venice*.
Before leaving Canada he played the lead in *Othello* at the
Crest Theatre; this was a role in which he had gained his
greatest fame in the English-speaking world. Mr Valk had
two careers; before 1939 he was a leading actor in Germany and in countries where German is spoken; as a Jew,
he fled from the Nazi regime to England, and there made
a new career, and gained new fame, acting in English.
Although he never spoke English without a perceptible
foreign accent he spoke it beautifully and eloquently.

As an actor, his strength lay in his powerful physique
which, with a splendid voice, fitted him for heroic roles.
He excelled in the representation of overwhelming passion;
his Othello was a whirlwind, ranging from the uttermost
violence of rage to moving depths of pathos. He was not
interested in subtleties, playing with great simplicity, but
he was able to do what so many actors cannot do—fill out
the great moments of overmastering passion. His Shylock
was a dignified, intensely human creation.

In private life he was a gentle, genial, humble man, easy

to work with and kind to beginners in his profession. It was a privilege to have him in Canada, and he will be sincerely mourned here.

PROGRAMMES

1955

Stratford Shakespearean Festival, Ontario

JULIUS CAESAR   Shakespeare

OEDIPUS REX   Sophocles

THE MERCHANT OF VENICE   Shakespeare

The Crest Theatre, Toronto

THEY KNEW WHAT THEY WANTED   Sidney Howard

OTHELLO   Shakespeare

STRATFORD SHAKESPEAREAN
FESTIVAL, ONTARIO, 1955

	JULIUS CAESAR	MERCHANT OF VENICE
FREDERICK VALK		Shylock
LORNE GREEN	Brutus	Prince of Morocco
DOUGLAS CAMPBELL	Casca	
LLOYD BOCHNER	Cassius	Salanio
ROBERT GOODIER	Octavius Officer	Antonio
ROBERT CHRISTIE	Julius Caesar	Duke
DONALD HARRON	Octavius Caesar	Bassanio
WILLIAM HUTT	Ligarius, Cinna (poet)	Old Gobbo
ERIC HOUSE	Claudius, Metellus	Prince of Aragon
DONALD DAVIS	Marcus Antonius	
DOUGLAS RAIN	Decius Brutus, Titinius	
EDWARD HOLMES	Cicero, Varro	Salarino
BRUNO GERUSSI	Marullus, Artemidorus, Pindarus	Tubal
TONY VAN BRIDGE	Messala, Cinna	
WILLIAM SHATNER	Lucius	Gratiano
TED FOLLOWS	Cobbler, Clitus	Launcelot Gobbo
BRUCE SWERDFAGER	Flavius, Dardanius	Balthasar
PETER HAWORTH	Volumnius	Antonio's servant
ROLAND BULL	Young Cato	Stephano
NEIL VIPOND	Antony Officer, Priest	Lorenzo
ROLAND HEWGILL	Soothsayer	
GRANT REDDICK	Trebonius	Leonardo
DAVID GARDNER	Popilius	
JOHN HAYES	Lepidus	
ALEX DE NAZRODY	Publius	
FRANCES HYLAND		Portia
ELEANOR STUART	Calpurnia	
BARBARA CHILCOTT	Portia	
HELEN BURNS		Nerissa
CHARLOTTE SCHRAGER		Jessica

JULIUS CAESAR	MERCHANT OF VENICE

Directed by

MICHAEL LANGHAM	TYRONE GUTHRIE

Designed by

TANYA MOISEIWITSCH

Music by

LOUIS APPLEBAUM	JOHN COOK

Citizens, Soldiers, Attendants:

Naomi Cameron, Aime Aunapuu, Roberta Kinnon, Gertrude Tyas, William Cole, Robin Gammell, John Gardiner, Robert Gibson, Richard Howard, John Horton, Charles Joliffe, Harry McGirt, Louis Negin, Peter Perehinczuk, Thurston Smith, Russell Waller, Alan Wilkinson, Barbara Franklin, Margaret Griffin, Irene Moszewska, Lynn Wilson, Joan Watts, Pauline Galbraith, Julian Flett, Orest Ulan, Bev Wilson, Allan Zielonka, Peter Henderson, Guy Belanger, Kenneth Paul, Jim Manser.

Elizabethan Singers:

Lloyd Bradshaw, Keith Elliot, John Boyden, Gordon Scott, Mrs Velda Scott, Mrs Helen Baumbach, Mrs Miriam Haines Root, Mrs Audrey Conroy, Mrs Eileen Hunter, Mrs Jean Moorehead.

STRATFORD SHAKESPEAREAN FESTIVAL, ONTARIO

KING OEDIPUS
by Sophocles

In a version by W. B. Yeats

Oedipus	Douglas Campbell
Priest	Eric House
Creon	Robert Goodier
Tiresias	Donald Davis
Jocasta	Eleanor Stuart
Man from Corinth	Tony van Bridge
Old Shepherd	Eric House
Chorus Leader	William Hutt

Chorus:
Roland Bull, Robert Christie, Ted Follows, David Gardner, Bruno Gerussi, Peter Haworth, John Hayes, Roland Hewgill, Edward Holmes, James Manser, Grant Reddick, William Shatner, Bruce Swerdfager, Neil Vipond.

Nurse	Gertrude Tyas
Ismene and Antigone	Nomi Cameron and Barbara Franklin

Attendants on Creon:
Orest Ulan, Bev Wilson, Julian Flett, Peter Henderson, John Horton, Harry McGirt.

Suppliants:
Aime Aunapuu, Guy Belanger, Nomi Cameron, William Cole, Barbara Franklin, Pauline Galbraith, Robin Gammell, John Gardiner, Robert Gibson, Margaret Griffin, Richard Howard, Charles Joliffe, Roberta Kinnon, Irene Moszewka, Alex de Nasrody, Louis Negin, Ken Pauli, Peter Perehinzuk, Thurston Smith, Gertrude Tyas, Russell Waller, Joan Watts, Allan Wilkinson, Lynn Wilson, Alan Zielonka.

Directed by
Tyrone Guthrie

Designed by
Tanya Moiseiwitsch

Music by
Cedric Thorpe Davie

THE CREST THEATRE, TORONTO

THEY KNEW WHAT THEY WANTED
by SIDNEY HOWARD

Joe	BRUNO GERUSSI
Father McKee	JAMES EDMOND
Ah Gee	GRAHAM PARKER
Tony	FREDERICK VALK
The R.F.D.	LLOYD JONES
Amy	JANET REID
Angelo	CHARLES HAYTER
Giorgio	EDWIN STEPHENSON
The Doctor	GRANT REDDICK

Directed by
BASIL COLEMAN

Setting and Costumes by
JOHN WILSON

THE CREST THEATRE, TORONTO

OTHELLO
by WILLIAM SHAKESPEARE

The Duke of Venice	ALAN NUNN
Brabantio—a Senator	TONY VAN BRIDGE
Other Senators	BRUCE SWERDFAGER
	JONATHAN WHITE
	CHARLES HAYTER
Othello—a General in the service of the Venetian State	FREDERICK VALK
Cassio—his Lieutenant	WILLIAM JOB
Iago—Othello's Ancient (Ensign)	MURRAY DAVIS
Roderigo—a Venetian	GRANT REDDICK
Ludovico—kinsman to Brabantio, Venetian Ambassador to Cyprus	ALAN NUNN
Montano—Acting-Governor of Cyprus	DAVID GARDNER
Gentlemen of Cyprus	BRUCE SWERDFAGER
	JONATHAN WHITE
	CHARLES HAYTER
Desdemona—daughter to Brabantio, wife to Othello	DIANA VANDERFLIS
Emilia—wife to Iago	BARBARA CHILCOTT
Bianca—mistress to Cassio	DEBORAH CASS

Soldiers:
Peter Henderson, Alan Zielonka, Keith Newman, Ron Hill, R. Brock
Shoveller, David Devall.

Directed by
BASIL COLEMAN

Setting by
JOHN WILSON

Costumes by
CLARENCE WILSON

Swordfights
JONATHAN WHITE

130

INDEX

INDEX

133